Telehealth Law Handbook: A Practical Guide to Virtual Care

First Edition

American Health
Lawyers Association

AMERICAN HEALTH LAWYERS ASSOCIATION
1620 Eye Street, NW, 6th Floor
Washington, DC 20006-4010
Web site: www.healthlawyers.org
E-Mail: info@healthlawyers.org

Printed in the United States of America

ISBN: 978-1-6328-1345-9 (Member print)

ISBN: 978-1-6328-1346-6 (Non-member print)

"This publication is designed to provide accurate and authoritative information with respect to the subject matter covered. It is provided with the understanding that the publisher is not engaged in rendering legal or other professional services. If legal advice or other expert assistance is required, the services of a competent professional person should be sought."

—from a declaration of the American Bar Association

AHLA Diversity+Inclusion Statement In principle and in practice, the American Health Lawyers Association values and seeks to advance and promote diverse and inclusive participation within the Association regardless of gender, race, ethnicity, religion, age, sexual orientation, gender identity and expression, national origin, or disability. Guided by these values, the Association strongly encourages and embraces participation of diverse individuals as it leads health law to excellence through education, information, and dialogue.

(Rel.1E Pub 29963)

Recent Titles from American Health Lawyers Association

Best Practices Handbook for Advising Clients on Fraud and Abuse Issues, First Edition

AHLA's Guide to Health Care Legal Forms, Agreements, and Policies, Second Edition with 2017 Cumulative Supplement

Federal Health Care Laws and Regulations, 2017–2018 Edition

The Fundamentals of Behavioral Health Care Law, First Edition

Enterprise Risk Management Handbook for Health Care Entities, Third Edition

Peer Review Guidebook, Fifth Edition

The Medical Staff Guidebook: Minimizing Risks and Maximizing Collaboration, Fourth Edition

Representing Hospitals and Health Systems Handbook, First Edition

Representing Physicians Handbook, Fourth Edition

Health Care Provider and Supplier Audits Practice Guide, First Edition

Health Plans Contracting Handbook: A Guide for Payers and Providers, Seventh Edition

Health Plan Disputes and Litigation Practice Guide, First Edition

Health Care Finance: A Primer, Third Edition

Data Breach Notification Laws: A Fifty State Survey, Second Edition

For more AHLA titles published with LexisNexis,
visit https://store.lexisnexis.com/ahla.

For more information on AHLA's ePrograms, webinar recordings and PDFs,
visit www.healthlawyers.org/store.

About the Authors

Jennifer R. Breuer (editor) is a partner at Drinker Biddle & Reath. She is vice chair of Drinker Biddle's Health Care Group and co-chair of the firm's Women's Leadership Committee. She represents health care providers and suppliers in transactional, compliance, and regulatory matters, with a focus on Stark Law and Anti-Kickback Statute compliance for hospital-physician relationships. Jen also advises on data strategy and privacy law compliance for electronic health records, health information exchanges, and other technology platforms. She regularly assists in the development of compliance strategies for ehealth and telemedicine providers. Prior to attending law school, Jen worked as a strategy consultant to the worldwide pharmaceutical, biotechnology, and medical device industries.

Soleil Teubner Boughton (Chapter 2) is corporate counsel at Google LLC, where she provides legal support for Google's health care product development efforts. Prior to joining Google, Soleil was a partner with Jones Day, where she represented health care and life sciences companies in connection with a broad variety of complex transactions and digital health matters. She has extensive experience advising both established and emerging companies with respect to telemedicine, telehealth, and other e-health topics, including direct-to-consumer telemedicine, eprescribing, provider-to-provider consults and second opinions, licensure, corporate structure and corporate practice of medicine issues, data privacy and security, remote supervision, provider contracting, and terms of use/privacy policy documentation. Ms. Boughton earned her J.D. from UCLA Law School and her B.A. from Pomona College.

Andrea Frey (Chapter 4) is an associate at Hooper, Lundy & Bookman, P.C. Her practice focuses on representing clients in the health care and life sciences industries in a wide range on transactional and regulatory matters. Andrea also regularly assists health care providers navigate requirements for patient privacy including HIPAA, patient medical records, electronic prescriptions, and information sharing between providers.

Jennifer Hansen (Chapter 4) is a partner at Hooper, Lundy & Bookman, P.C. and the first chair of her firm's Medical Staff Work Group. Her practice includes representation of hospitals, medical staffs, post-acute care providers, pharmacies, and other health care providers and suppliers in a wide range of matters, including civil and administrative health care litigation, medical staff law, managed care litigation, licensing, reimbursement, long term care surveys and appeals, and other regulatory matters. She is currently the Social Media Chair for the Medical Staff, Credentialing, and Peer Review Practice Group for AHLA. Ms. Hansen is a past Co-Chair of the San Diego County Bar Association Law & Medicine Section and Lawyers Club Community Outreach Committee. Ms. Hansen earned her B.A. from the University of Wisconsin, Madison with honors, and her J.D. from the University of Minnesota Law School.

Nathaniel Lacktman (Chapter 3) is a partner and health care lawyer with the law firm Foley & Lardner LLP. He is the Chair of the firm's Telemedicine and Virtual Care Practice and Co-Chair of the firm's Digital Health Group. He advises hospitals, health care providers, and technology companies on business arrangements, compliance, and corporate matters, with particular attention to telehealth, digital health, and health innovation. His approach to practicing law emphasizes strategic counseling, creative business modeling, and fresh approaches to realize clients' ambitious and innovative goals. He serves on the Executive Committee of the American Telemedicine Association's Business & Finance Group, co-chairs the Telemedicine and eHealth Affinity Group of the American Health Lawyers Association, and serves as Chief Legal Counsel to the Telehealth Association of Florida. Mr. Lacktman speaks and writes frequently on issues at the forefront of telehealth, and has helped author telemedicine policy letters and position statements with such organizations as the American Telemedicine Association and the American Heart Association. He has provided comments, draft legislation, and policy input on telehealth to state lawmakers, the Drug Enforcement Agency, the Congressional Research Service, state Medicaid Agencies, and state boards of medicine. He has appeared in publications such as *Modern Healthcare*, *Forbes*, *Fox News*, *Bloomberg*, *Reuters*, *Associated Press*, *Inside Counsel*, *Buzzfeed*, *Politico*, and *Information Week* among others. He is a graduate of the University of Southern California School of Law and the University of Florida.

Vivek J. Rao (Chapter 1) is a member of Pierce Atwood's Business and Intellectual Property practice groups. He focuses on technology and intellectual property transactions, the protection and enforcement of trademark and other intellectual property rights, and data privacy and security matters, including advising health care clients regarding HIPAA and other privacy and security issues. Before joining Pierce Atwood, Vivek maintained a litigation practice with Zuckerman Spaeder LLP in Washington, D.C.

Emily Wein (Chapter 2) is a principal in the Baker Ober Health Law Group of Baker Donelson. She advises on a wide spectrum of regulatory considerations affecting clients engaged in telemedicine, whether they are the telemedicine service provider or telemedicine service recipient. Such issues include the federal fraud and abuse requirements (both anti-kickback and Stark law), HIPAA privacy, Medicare and Medicaid payment, medical staff credentialing, state licensure, and corporate practice of medicine considerations. She also assists clients with their Medicare enrollment matters and health care facility licensure issues. She was previously Associate Counsel at a large interdisciplinary health system where assisted in the expansion of the organization's telemedicine offerings as well as served as primary regulatory counsel in the area of fraud and abuse and HIPAA compliance.

About the Authors

Christine Burke Worthen (Chapter 1), Chair of Pierce Atwood's Healthcare Services Practice Group, focuses her practice on health care law and ERISA and employee benefits law. Christine guides health care organizations on managed care contracting, accountable care organizations, risk based contracting, network design, telemedicine, health privacy and security laws (including HIPAA), and the 340b federal drug pricing program. Christine has experience in the transition from volume to value based reimbursement and provides counsel to health care organizations that participate in the Medicare Shared Savings Program, the Pioneer ACO Program, the Next Generation ACO Model, and risk arrangements with commercial payors. She also provides counsel to independent physician practices facing changing reimbursement models.

Christine provides legal and strategic guidance on high performing clinically integrated network design and development as well as the integration and use of data necessary to succeed in value based reimbursement models. She also provides counsel to health care organizations in the design and implementation of telemedicine programs and guides on compliance with the various state and federal laws that impact telemedicine such as state licensure, scope of practice, reimbursement, privacy and security, fraud and abuse, and contracting. Christine also assists self-funded employers with health plan design and network development to promote value-based benefit designs. She drafts and guides on executive compensation plans, retirement plans, health and welfare benefit plans, and health care reform issues.

Before joining Pierce Atwood, Christine was associate general counsel for Eastern Maine Healthcare Systems, where she provided guidance in all areas of health care law and ERISA/employee benefits issues.

Yanyan Zhou (Chapter 4) is an associate at Hooper, Lundy & Bookman, P.C. She represents health care providers and suppliers in transactional, compliance and regulatory matters, with a focus on licensing, reimbursement and compliance. Yanyan also advises clients on professional scope of practice issues. Prior to law school, Yanyan worked in the pharmaceutical industry.

Acknowledgements

Jennifer Hansen

Thanks Thomas Wm. Mayo and Tara E. Kepler, the authors of the 2007 book, *Telemedicine: Survey and Analysis of Federal and State Laws*, which served as an inspiration for this publication and a foundation for portions of her chapter.

Nathaniel Lacktman

To my wife, Malloy, and children, Oliver and Bennett, for their love and support. To Judy Waltz, my colleague and mentor, for the encouragement to publish and speak on health law (and who must be smiling at my "vow" never to write another book chapter). To Patricia Markus and Alexis Gilroy, for extending the invitation to serve my first leadership role with AHLA and welcoming me to the fold. And finally, to Will Harvey, for reviving this book concept and bringing together this talented group of authors and editors.

About the American Health Lawyers Association

Leading health law to excellence through education, information, and dialogue, the American Health Lawyers Association (AHLA) is the nation's largest, nonpartisan, 501(c)(3) educational organization devoted to legal issues in the health care field with nearly 14,000 members.

The mission of the American Health Lawyers Association is to provide a collegial forum for interaction and information exchange to enable its members to serve their clients more effectively; to produce the highest quality non-partisan educational programs, products, and services concerning health law issues; and to serve as a public resource on selected health care legal issues.

AHLA provides resources to address the issues facing its active members who practice in law firms, government, in-house settings and academia and who represent the entire spectrum of the health industry: physicians, hospitals and health systems, health maintenance organizations, health insurers, life sciences entities, managed care companies, nursing facilities, home care providers, and consumers.

Table of Contents

Introduction

Telehealth is changing relationships not only between physicians and patients, but also among providers, and between providers and payers. As state and federal legislators and regulators take note of these changed relationships, the law is changing as well.

The American Health Lawyers Association is pleased to bring you this *Telehealth Law Handbook: A Practical Guide to Virtual Care* to help you navigate the highly dynamic and state-law dependent practice of telehealth.

This book examines how the law impacts all manner of telehealth relationships. Chapter One examines telemedicine licensure requirements in all 50 states, including a discussion of types of state licensure, exceptions, and how licensure laws apply in particular practice situations, such as physician-to-physician consultations and physician-patient visits.

Chapter Two describes telehealth regulatory requirements, beginning with an examination of telehealth practice and communication models and analyzing the application of state regulation on the physician-patient relationship, validation of identity, informed consent, vulnerable populations, nonphysician providers, remote prescribing, and continuity of care.

Chapter Three addresses payment and reimbursement considerations, including telehealth payment and reimbursement rules under Medicare and Medicaid programs, emerging state laws known as telehealth commercial insurance and payment parity statutes, and a 50-state survey of state telehealth commercial insurance coverage laws.

Chapter Four analyzes other emerging legal and ethical issues, including a discussion of important telehealth considerations such as medical staff credentialing, ethics and liability issues, fraud and abuse compliance, corporate practice of medicine prohibitions, privacy and security issues, and mobile health technology.

We trust you will find this book useful in developing your understanding of the complex rules surrounding this method of health care delivery.

Chapter 1

Licensing

1.1 Introduction

As the U.S. health care delivery system evolves from volume-based reimbursement to value-based reimbursement, traditional fragmented models of care have eroded in favor of models that focus on high-quality, lower-cost, patient-centered care that is coordinated across the continuum. Patients are increasingly regarded as consumers with whom providers must develop a relationship through engagement and improved access to health care services. There is an increased focus on interoperability in health care technology platforms as well as data driven approaches to patient care, both of which require coordination and removal of traditional barriers to integration. With the potential to increase quality and access, lower costs, and foster patient engagement, telehealth plays a key role in the evolving health care delivery landscape. Despite its potential and increased presence, the numerous state licensing requirements that physicians must contend with present challenges to telehealth adoption.

Historically, physicians did not need to be concerned with practicing across state lines: they provided care face-to-face to patients located only in the single state in which they were domiciled. This traditional approach has been undergoing substantial change as hospital systems and physician practices increasingly cross state lines. Further, improved technology has made it possible to reduce barriers to accessing care by delivering services via telehealth, whether emergency consults, second opinions, or routine virtual visits to patients in rural areas.

Telehealth helps to remove socioeconomic barriers to care, such as patients—and their parents and caregivers—having to miss work in order to visit a provider office, or having to pay for child care to attend in-person appointments, or not having access to convenient or affordable transportation. Telehealth also aids in delivering care as we face an increased shortage of physicians.

As a general rule, when patients are located in another state, the licensing focus is on the site of the delivery of care, i.e., the state in which the patient is located. "Telemedicine" is often still used when referring to traditional clinical diagnosis and monitoring that is delivered by technology. However, the term "telehealth" is now more commonly used as it describes the wide range of diagnosis and management, education, and other health care service that may be provided using technology. This chapter will examine the current state of telehealth/telemedicine licensure in the 50 states, including licensure requirements and exceptions, efforts to streamline licensure across states, and considerations for multistate practice.

1.2 Current State of Telemedicine Licensure—State-by-State Analysis Required

There is no uniform approach to state licensing for telehealth services. Thus, for physicians wishing to practice across state lines, state-by-state analysis of licensure requirements is necessary. From a licensing perspective, the requirements can be broken down into categories: (a) states that expressly subject out-of-state physicians practicing across state lines to full licensure requirements; (b) states that permit such physicians to practice across state lines using a special purpose license; and (c) states whose licensure statutes and regulations do not separately address telehealth. Some states also offer licensure via reciprocity or limited licensure. Further, many states offer a consultation exception, which permits physician-to-physician consults rather than direct patient contact or permits physicians to provide consults to patients that are in the nature of second opinions, rather than medical orders. The Interstate Medical Licensure Compact, a voluntary, expedited pathway for multistate licensure, may provide a solution to the time-consuming and burdensome process of obtaining licenses in multiple states. Keep in mind that licensure is just one of the issues physicians need to consider. Once a license is obtained, the physician will still need to comply with the state medical practice acts and applicable practice standards. Practice standards are discussed in Section 2.5.2.

1.2.1 States with Full Licensure Requirements

Most states require physicians to obtain regular licenses to practice medicine for the provision of telehealth and/or telehealth services. Some states specifically address the provision of telemedicine services in their state in their licensing statutes. For example, Wyoming defines telemedicine as "the practice of medicine by electronic communication or other means from a physician in a location to a patient in another location, with or without an intervening health care provider;"[1] Colorado includes "[t]he delivery of telemedicine" within the definition of "practice of medicine."[2] On the other hand, other states do not directly address telemedicine or telehealth in their licensing requirements. Absent an exception, one should assume that full licensure is required to provide telehealth services in those states, assuming those services fall within the purview of the practice of medicine. See Table 1.1 for further details.

1.2.2 States with Special License Requirements

Rather than imposing full licensure requirements on the practice of telehealth, a handful of states, such as Minnesota, have special licensure requirements for telehealth. Minnesota allows physicians who are licensed in another state but not in Minnesota to "provide medical services to a patient located in this state through interstate telemedicine if the following conditions are met: (1) the physician is licensed without restriction to practice medicine in the state from which the physician provides telemedicine services; (2) the physician has not had a license to practice medicine revoked or restricted in any state or jurisdiction; (3) the physician does not open an office in this state, does not meet with patients in this state, and does not receive calls in this state from patients; and (4) the physician annually registers with the board, on a form provided by the board."[3] Minnesota qualifies this special licensing requirement with the caveat that if the telemedicine services are provided on an "infrequent" basis, then the licensing requirements do not apply.[4]

As of January 1, 2017, ten states maintain special licensing requirements specific to telehealth (whether described as "telehealth," "telemedicine," or "practice of medicine across state lines").[5] Tennessee now requires only a special purpose license for doctors of osteopathy, and Montana and Nevada have adopted the Federation of State Medical Boards' Interstate Medical Licensure Compact, which is discussed in Section 1.2.4.[6] Alabama's Board of Medical Examiners repealed some of its telehealth rules in 2015, including its practice standards for a special purpose license for telehealth. See Table 1.1 for further details.

---

[1] Wyo. Stat. § 33-26-102.

[2] Colo. Rev. Stat. § 12-36-106(1)(g).

[3] Minn. Stat. Ann. § 147.032.

[4] Minn. Stat. Ann. § 147.032.

[5] The ten states are: Alabama, Louisiana, Maine, Minnesota, Nevada, New Mexico, Ohio, Oregon, Tennessee, and Texas.

[6] *State Telehealth Laws and Medicaid Program Policies*, Public Health Institute Center for Connected Health Policy, August 2016.

1.2.3 States with Bordering State Exceptions

The concept of bordering state licensing exceptions is an option in a few states, which reduces the licensing burden on physicians. Three states and the District of Columbia have enacted language to facilitate licensure reciprocity from bordering states.[7] For example, Maryland excepts from its licensure requirements physicians who are duly licensed in the bordering states of Virginia, West Virginia, Delaware, and Pennsylvania.[8]

1.2.4 Interstate Medical Licensure Compact

The Interstate Medical Licensure Compact (IML Compact) offers a voluntary, expedited pathway to licensure for qualified physicians who wish to practice in multiple states. This approach is intended to increase access to health care for patients in underserved or rural areas by fostering opportunities to connect with medical providers through telehealth. By making it easier for physicians to obtain licenses to practice in multiple states, the IML Compact would foster the ability of states to share investigative and disciplinary information, thereby protecting the public. As of 2017, the IML Compact has been enacted by legislation in eighteen states,[9] with legislation pending in five additional states.[10] The IML Compact is in the process of establishing its administrative process for expedited licensure, which is expected to be available soon.

To be eligible for expedited licensure under the IML Compact, physicians must:

- Possess a full and unrestricted license to practice medicine in an IML Compact state;
- Possess specialty certification or be in possession of a time unlimited specialty certificate;
- Have no discipline on any state medical license;
- Have no discipline related to controlled substances;
- Not be under investigation by any licensing or law enforcement agency;
- Have passed the USMLE or COMLEX (or equivalent) within three attempts; and
- Have successfully completed a graduate medical education program.

Physicians who are ineligible for the expedited licensure process facilitated by the IML Compact will still be able to seek additional licenses in those states in which they desire to practice using the traditional state-by-state licensure processes. Facilitating expedited medical licensure through the IML Compact ensures that states retain their role in regulating the practice of medicine and protecting patient welfare. The IML Compact represents the efforts of the adopting states to develop a system of expedited licensure over which such states can maintain control through a coordinated legislative and administrative process.

1.2.5 Physician-to-Physician/Infrequent Consultations and Other Limited Exceptions to Licensure

Many states carve out exceptions for the provision of telehealth services under specified circumstances. Many states have exceptions to their general requirement for licensure that applies to physician-to-physician consultation. Those states generally require the out-of-state physician to be duly licensed in the state in which such physician is located and resides, the in-state physician

[7] The three states in addition to the District of Columbia are: Maryland, New York, and Virginia.

[8] Md. Code, Health Occ. § 14-302.

[9] The eighteen states are: Alabama, Arizona, Colorado, Idaho, Illinois, Iowa, Kansas, Minnesota, Mississippi, Montana, Nevada, New Hampshire, Pennsylvania, South Dakota, Utah, West Virginia, Wisconsin, and Wyoming.

[10] The five states are: Arkansas, Michigan, Nebraska, North Dakota, and Washington.

to be duly licensed in the state in which the patient is located and to maintain the physician-patient relationship, and the nature of the services provided to be in the form of a second opinion or a consultation. Some states have exceptions for "infrequent" practice across state lines, in some cases limited to consultations, but in others, such as Alabama,[11] not so limited. Other states, like Washington,[12] have exceptions that do not turn on frequency or type of service but include other requirements, such as not opening an office in the state.

1.2.5.1 Physician-to-Physician Consultations

Several large health systems advertise second opinion services whereby their physicians will provide a remote second opinion to a physician in another state. Various states facilitate the provision of these services via exceptions to general licensing requirements for physician-to-physician consults. Of those states that permit physician-to-physician consultations, a few permit direct patient contact so long as it is either infrequent or at the direction of the in-state physician. Regardless of the specifics of the exception, responsibility for patient care always rests with the in-state physician.

A number of the consultation exceptions are broadly defined. Alaska, for example, provides that its licensing laws do not apply to "a physician or osteopath, who is not a resident of this state, who is asked by a physician or osteopath licensed in this state to help in the diagnosis or treatment of a case."[13] Massachusetts similarly provides that its licensing and registration requirements "shall not apply . . . to a physician or surgeon resident in another state who is a legal practitioner therein, when in actual consultation with a legal practitioner of the commonwealth."[14] It should be noted that some of the otherwise broadly defined exceptions might be read narrowly to require *in-person* consultation. For example, Florida exempts from licensure requirements out-of-state physicians "*meeting* duly licensed physicians of this state in consultation,"[15] and Kansas exempts "[p]ractitioners of the healing arts licensed in another state when and while incidentally *called into* this state in consultation with practitioners licensed in this state."[16] In considering such statutes, it may be prudent to consult local counsel and/or contact the relevant state licensing board to obtain additional clarity as to whether the exception is interpreted as reaching practice across state lines.

Some states limit their physician-to-physician consultation exceptions to particular types of consultations. For example, Louisiana excepts from its licensure a "true consultation, e.g., an informal consultation or second opinion;"[17] Michigan limits its exception to consultations obtained "in an exceptional circumstance;"[18] and Texas permits consultation services without Texas licensure only when provided by a "medical specialist."[19] Other states, like Alabama[20] and Ohio,[21] require that the consultation occur without compensation to (i) either physician, in the case of Alabama, or (ii) the physician providing the consultation, in the case of Ohio.

---

[11] Ala. Code § 34-24-505(b).

[12] Wash. Rev. Code § 18.71.030(6).

[13] Alaska Stat. 08.64.370.

[14] Mass. Gen. Laws ch. 112, § 7.

[15] Fla. Stat. § 458.303(1)(b) (emphasis added).

[16] Kan. Stat. § 65-2872(j) (emphasis added).

[17] 46 La. Admin. Code § 7515(A)(1).

[18] Mich. Comp. Laws § 333.16171(e).

[19] Tex. Admin. Code § 172.12(f)(1); *see also* Tex. Occ. Code § 151.056(b)(1).

[20] Ala. Code § 34-24-501(a)(3).

[21] Ohio Rev. Code § 4731.36(A)(3)(b).

A number of states limit the physician-to-physician consultation exception to consultations that occur on an infrequent basis, do not last beyond a threshold duration, or both. For example, Arizona,[22] Connecticut,[23] and Georgia,[24] exempt from licensure requirements only "infrequent" or "irregular" or "occasional" consultations, without expressly defining those terms, potentially creating uncertainty as to when licensure is actually required. Other states have expressly established thresholds. In Iowa, for example, one of the requirements to achieve the consultation exception is that the consulting physician "practices in Iowa for a period not greater than 10 consecutive days and not more than 20 total days in any calendar year."[25]

Still other states condition their physician-to-physician consultation exceptions on the out-of-state physician not opening an office or receiving calls in the relevant state. For example, California requires that the out-of-state physician "not open an office, appoint a place to meet patients, receive calls from patients within the limits of this state, give orders, or have ultimate authority over the care or primary diagnosis of a patient who is located within this state."[26]

See Table 1.2 for a complete state-by-state list of physician-to-physician consultation exceptions to licensure requirements, categorized into exceptions that are expressly conditioned on the nature of the consultation, exceptions that are expressly conditioned on the frequency of the consultation, exceptions that are expressly conditioned on the nature and frequency of the consultation, and exceptions that do not have any significant conditions (other than the existence of a consultation with a licensed in-state physician). The Table also lists some exceptions that are not specific to physician-to-physician consultations but may have some applicability in that context. Please note this supplementary list is not exhaustive.

1.2.5.2 Infrequent Consultations and Other Limited Exceptions

The handful of states that offer general exceptions to their licensing requirements for direct-to-patient consultations do so in a variety of ways. They can offer a broad exception for second opinions or limit the scope to "infrequent" consultations or consultations provided by physicians who do not maintain an office in the state or take calls in the state. Colorado, for example, does not require licensure for out-of-state physicians limiting their services in Colorado to "an occasional case or consultation," provided that such physicians satisfy a number of other requirements, including maintaining out-of-state licensure, not entering into any contract, agreement, or understanding to provide services in Colorado on a regular or routine basis, not maintaining an office or other place for the rendering of such services, and maintaining medical liability insurance coverage in the amounts required under Colorado law.[27] Minnesota provides that "a physician who is not licensed to practice medicine in this state, but who holds a valid license to practice medicine in another state or jurisdiction, and who provides interstate telemedicine services to a patient located in this state is not subject to the registration requirement . . . if: (2) the services are provided on an irregular or infrequent basis. For the purposes of this section, a person provides services on an irregular or infrequent basis if the person provides the services less than once a month or provides the services to fewer than ten patients annually; or (3) the physician provides interstate telemedicine

---

[22] Ariz. Rev. Stat. § 32-1421(B)(1).

[23] Conn. Gen. Stat. § 20-9(d).

[24] Ga. Code § 43-34-31(b)(1).

[25] Iowa Admin. Code § 653-9.1.

[26] Cal. Bus. & Prof. Code § 2060.

[27] Colo. Rev. Stat. § 12-36-106(3)(b).

services in this state in consultation with a physician licensed in this state and the Minnesota physician retains ultimate authority over the diagnosis and care of the patient."[28]

1.2.6 Other Requirements: In Person Visits and Satisfying Physician-Patient Requirements via Telehealth

States take a variety of approaches for in-person versus telemedicine visits before, during, and after a patient encounter. Some states impose stricter standards for physicians when using telemedicine, and may require in-person visits in addition to a telemedicine evaluation. Other states permit the telemedicine visit to satisfy the in-person requirement. Such policies affect a physician's licensure status and ability to practice medicine. For example, Alaska provides that disciplinary sanctions may not be imposed on a physician for "rendering a diagnosis, providing treatment, or prescribing, dispensing, or administering a prescription drug that is not a controlled substance to a person without conduct a physical examination if: (1) the physician or another licensed health care provider or physician in the physician's group practice is available to provide follow-up care; and (2) the physician requests that the person consent to sending a copy of all records of the encounter to the person's primary care provider if the prescribing physician is not the person's primary care provider, and if the patient consents, the physician sends the records to the person's primary care provider."[29] The Alaska Medical Board is required to adopt regulations establishing guidelines for a physician who renders a diagnosis, provides treatment, or prescribes, dispenses, or administers a prescription drug without conducting a physical examination.[30]

1.2.7 State Licensure Differences: Other Issues

In addition to differences among the states in terms of licensure requirements, one needs to keep in mind that other differences exist from a licensing perspective. These include differences in defining what constitutes the practice of medicine or telemedicine, additional licensure requirements for supervision of other practitioners, varying approaches to informing patients, and continuity of care. Physicians need to be mindful that the complications of obtaining licensure may be no less than ensuring compliance with maintenance requirements.

1.2.8 Other Issues: Nurses

With the increased focus on care coordination and care management under value-based reimbursement models and the development of team-based approaches to primary care (which often focus on the role of nurses as part of a multidisciplinary team), multistate telemedicine models need to take into account nurse licensure issues as well. Value-based care incorporates such concepts as patient-centered medical homes and accountable care models, in which patient care continues to move away from episodic, fragmented care to care that is managed across the continuum. Nurse care managers play a key role in patient follow-up and patient engagement. They may follow patients with multiple comorbidities to ensure they adhere to care plans, or they may follow patients after discharge from a hospital to ensure that the patients have appropriate follow-up appointments and resources to reduce readmissions. Telehealth plays an important role in the delivery of these services, from remote patient monitoring to virtual visits.

From a state licensing perspective, the Nurse Licensure Compact (Nurse Compact), allows nurses who reside in a Nurse Compact state to practice in other Nurse Compact states under one multistate license. The nurse must follow the nurse licensure act of each state and is subject to discipline in the states of practice. If a nurse wishes to practice in a non-Nurse-Compact state, or relocates to a

---

[28] Minn. Stat. § 147.032.

[29] Alaska Stat. § 08.64.364.

[30] Alaska Stat. § 08.64.101.

non-Nurse-Compact state, the nurse must apply for single-state licensure by endorsement. If a nurse moves to another Nurse Compact state, the nurse can retain the multistate license via endorsement. States become Nurse Compact members through legislation; there is model legislation available to adopt the Nurse Compact. At the present time, twenty-five states have adopted the Nurse Compact.[31]

The Enhanced Nurse Licensure Compact (Enhanced Compact) was rolled out in 2015. The Enhanced Compact added additional requirements to achieve licensure, such as a required criminal background check (state and federal) on initial licensure and prohibitions on acquiring a multistate license if a nurse is ever convicted of a felony. The Enhanced Compact will take effect upon adoption by twenty-six states or the end of 2018, whichever is earlier.

As of June 2017, Enhanced Compact legislation had been enacted in twenty-three states and was pending in five more.[32]

Table 1.1 Applicability of State Medical Licensure Requirements to Interstate Telemedicine

Table 1.1: Applicability of State Medical Licensure Requirements to Interstate Telemedicine			
Alabama	Ala. Code §§ 34-24-50, 34-24-51, 34-24-501, 34-24-502; Ala. Admin. Code 540-X-16.	**Full or Special Purpose License Required**	The practice of medicine or osteopathy across state lines means the practice of medicine or osteopathy as defined in Section 34-24-50(1), as it applies to: (1) The rendering of a written or otherwise documented medical opinion concerning the diagnosis or treatment of a patient located within this state by a physician located outside this state as a result of transmission of individual patient data by electronic or other means from within this state to such physician or his or her agent; or (2) The rendering of treatment to a patient located within this state by a physician located outside this state as a result of transmission of individual patient data by electronic or other means from this state to such physician or his or her agent. Ala. Code § 34-24-502(a); *see also* Ala. Admin. Code 540-X-16-.02.
Alaska	Alaska Stat. §§ 08.64.170, 08.64.360, 08.64.370.	**Telemedicine Not Directly Addressed**	
Arizona	Ariz. Rev. Stat. § 32-1401(22).	**Telemedicine Not Directly Addressed**	

[31] The twenty-five states are: Arizona, Arkansas, Colorado, Delaware, Idaho, Iowa, Kentucky, Maine, Maryland, Mississippi, Missouri, Montana, Nebraska, New Hampshire, New Mexico, North Carolina, North Dakota, Rhode Island, South Carolina, South Dakota, Tennessee, Texas, Utah, Virginia, and Wisconsin.

[32] The twenty-three states that had enacted Enhanced Compact legislation were: Arizona, Arkansas, Florida, Georgia, Idaho, Iowa, Kentucky, Maryland, Mississippi, Missouri, Montana, Nebraska, New Hampshire, North Dakota, Oklahoma, South Carolina, South Dakota, Tennessee, Texas, Utah, Virginia, West Virginia, and Wyoming. The states with pending Enhanced Compact legislation were: Delaware, Maine, Massachusetts, New Jersey, and North Carolina. For an updated summary of enacted and pending legislation, visit www.nursecompact.com.

Table 1.1: Applicability of State Medical Licensure Requirements to Interstate Telemedicine			
Arkansas	Ark. Code §§ 17-95-206, 17-95-401.	**Full License Required**	A physician who is physically located outside this state but who through the use of any medium, including an electronic medium, performs an act that is part of a patient care service initiated in this state, including the performance or interpretation of an X-ray examination or the preparation or interpretation of pathological material that would affect the diagnosis or treatment of the patient, is engaged in the practice of medicine in this state for the purposes of this chapter [concerning physicians and surgeons] and is subject to this chapter and to appropriate regulation by the Arkansas State Medical Board. Ark. Code § 17-95-206.
California	Cal. Bus. & Prof. Code § 2052.	**Telemedicine Not Directly Addressed**	
Colorado	Colo. Rev. Stat. § 12-36-106.	**Full License Required**	The term "telemedicine" is used but not expressly defined: "[P]ractice of medicine" includes "[t]he delivery of telemedicine." Colo. Rev. Stat. § 12-36-106(1)(g).
Connecticut	Conn. Gen. Stat. § 20-9	**Full License Required**	The provisions of subsection (a) of this section [concerning licensure] shall apply to any individual whose practice of medicine includes any ongoing, regular or contractual arrangement whereby, regardless of residency in this or any other state, he provides, through electronic communications or interstate commerce, diagnostic or treatment services, including primary diagnosis of pathology specimens, slides or images, to any person located in this state. Conn. Gen. Stat. § 20-9(d).
Delaware	24 Del. Code §§ 1702(11), 1720(a).	**Full License Required**	"Practice of medicine" . . . includes . . . [r]endering a written or otherwise documented medical opinion concerning the diagnosis or treatment of a person or the actual rendering of treatment to a person within the State by a physician located outside the State as a result of transmission of the person's medical data by electronic or other means from within the State to the physician or to the physician's agent[.] 24 Del. Code § 1702(11)(e).
District of Columbia	D.C. Code §§ 3-1201.02(7), 3-1205.01, 3-1210.01.	**Full License Required**	"Practice of medicine" . . . include[s] . . . [r]endering a written or otherwise documented medical opinion relating to the diagnosis and treatment of a person within the District, or the actual rendering of treatment to a person within the District, by a physician located outside the District as a result of transmission of the person's medical data by electronic or other means from within the District to the physician or to the physician's agent. D.C. Code § 3-1201.02(7)(A)(v).
Florida	Fla. Stat. §§ 456.065, 458.305(3), 458.327(1)(a), 458.3255.	**Telemedicine Not Directly Addressed**	

Table 1.1: Applicability of State Medical Licensure Requirements to Interstate Telemedicine			
Georgia	Ga. Code §§ 43-34-21(3), 43-34-26(a), 43-34-31(a).	**Full License Required**	A person who is physically located in another state . . . and who, through the use of any means, including electronic, radiographic, or other means of telecommunication, through which medical information or data are transmitted, performs and act that is part of a patient care service located in this state, including but not limited to the initiation of imaging procedures or the preparation of pathological material for examination, and that would affect the diagnosis or treatment of the patient is engaged in the practice of medicine in this state. Any person who performs such acts through such means shall be required to have a license to practice medicine in this state and shall be subject to regulation by the board. Any such out-of-state . . . practitioner shall not have ultimate authority over the care or primary diagnosis of a patient who is located in this state. Ga. Code § 43-34-31(a).
Hawaii	Haw. Rev. Stat. §§ 453-1.3, 453-2.	**Full License Required**	A physician shall not use telehealth to establish a physician-patient relationship with a patient in this State without a license to practice medicine in Hawaii. Haw. Rev. Stat. § 453-1.3(e). Once a provider-patient relationship is established, a patient or physician licensed in this State may use telehealth for any purpose, including consultation with a medical provider licensed in another state, authorized by this section or as otherwise provided by law. *Id.* § 453-1.3(f). "Telehealth" means the use of telecommunications as that term is defined in section 269-1, to encompass four modalities: store and forward technologies, remote monitoring, live consultation, and mobile health; and which shall include but not be limited to real-time video conferencing-based communication, secure interactive and non-interactive web-based communication, and secure asynchronous information exchange, to transmit patient medical information, including diagnostic-quality digital images and laboratory results for medical interpretation and diagnosis, for the purposes of: delivering enhanced health care services and information while a patient is at an originating site and the physician is at a distant site; establishing a physician-patient relationship; evaluating a patient; or treating a patient. *Id.*§ 453-1.
Idaho	Idaho Code §§ 54-1803(1), 54-1804.	**Telemedicine Not Directly Addressed**	

Table 1.1: Applicability of State Medical Licensure Requirements to Interstate Telemedicine			
Illinois	225 Ill. Comp. Stat. §§ 60/3, 60/49.5(b), (c).	**Full License Required**	For purpose of this Act, "telemedicine" means the performance of any of the activities listed in Section 49 [requiring medical license for various activities], including but not limited to rendering written or oral opinions concerning diagnosis or treatment of a patient in Illinois by a person located outside the State of Illinois as a result of transmission of individual patient data by telephonic, electronic, or other means of communication from within this State. 225 Ill. Comp. Stat. § 60/49.5(c).
Indiana	Ind. Code §§ 25-22.5-1-1.1(a)(4), 25-22.5-8-1.	**Full License Required**	"Practice of medicine or osteopathic medicine" includes "[p]roviding diagnostic or treatment services to a person in Indiana when the diagnostic or treatment services: (A) are transmitted through electronic communications; and (B) are on a regular, routine, and nonepisodic basis or under an oral or written agreement to regularly provide medical services." Ind. Code § 25-22.5-1.1(a)(4).
Iowa	Iowa Code §§ 147.2, 148.1.	**Telemedicine Not Directly Addressed**	
Kansas	Kan. Stat. §§ 65-2802(a), 65-2803(a).	**Telemedicine Not Directly Addressed**	
Kentucky	Ky. Rev. Stat. §§ 311.550(10), 311.560(1).	**Telemedicine Not Directly Addressed**	
Louisiana	La. Rev. Stat. §§ 37:1262(3)-(4), 1271, 1276.1, 1284.	**Full or Special Purpose License Required**	"Telemedicine" means the practice of health care delivery, diagnosis, consultation, treatment, and transfer of medical data using interactive telecommunication technology that enables a health care practitioner and a patient at two locations separated by distance to interact via two-way video and audio transmissions simultaneously. Neither a telephone conversation nor an electronic mail message between a health care practitioner and patient, or a true consultation as may be defined by rules promulgated by the board pursuant to the Administrative Procedure Act, constitutes telemedicine for purposes of this Part. La. Rev. Stat. § 37:1262(4).
Maine	32 Me. Rev. Stat. §§ 3270, 3300-D.	**Full or Special Purpose License Required**	"[T]elemedicine," as it pertains to the delivery of health care services, means the use of interactive audio, video or other electronic media for the purpose of diagnosis, consultation or treatment. "Telemedicine" does not include the use of audio-only telephone, facsimile machine or e-mail. 24-A Me. Rev. Stat. § 4316(1); *see also* 32 Me. Rev. Stat. 3300-D(1); *but see* 02-373-1 Code Me. R. § 1(10) ("Telemedicine" [means] [t]he practice of medicine at a distance through the use of any electronic means.).
Maryland	Md. Code, Health Occ. §§ 14-101(l), (o), 14-301.	**Telemedicine Not Directly Addressed**	

Table 1.1: Applicability of State Medical Licensure Requirements to Interstate Telemedicine			
Massachusetts	Mass. Gen. Laws ch. 112, § 6; 243 Mass. Code Regs. § 2.01(4).	**Full License Required**	Telemedicine is the provision of services to a patient by a physician from a distance by electronic communication in order to improve patient care, treatment or services. 243 Mass. Code Regs. § 2.01(4).
Michigan	Mich. Comp. Laws §§ 333.17001, 333.17011(1).	**Telemedicine Not Directly Addressed**	
Minnesota	Minn. Stat. §§ 147.032, 147.081.	**Full or Special Purpose License Required**	[T]elemedicine means the practice of medicine as defined in section 147.081, subdivision 3, when the physician is not in the physical presence of the patient. Minn. Stat. § 147.032-1(e).
Mississippi	Miss. Code §§ 73-25-1, 73-25-34.	**Full License Required**	[T]elemedicine, or the practice of medicine across state lines, shall be defined to include any one or both of the following: (a) Rendering of a medical opinion concerning diagnosis or treatment of a patient within this state by a physician located outside this state as a result of transmission of individual patient data by electronic or other means from within this state to such physician or his agent; or (b) The rendering of treatment to a patient within this state by a physician located outside this state as a result of transmission of individual patient data by electronic or other means from within this state to such physician or his agent. Miss. Code. § 73-25-34(1).
Missouri	Mo. Rev. Stat. § 334.010.	**Full License Required**	The "practice of medicine across state lines" shall mean: (1) The rendering of a written or otherwise documented medical opinion concerning the diagnosis or treatment of a patient within this state by a physician located outside this state as a result of transmission of individual patient data by electronic or other means from within this state to such physician or physician's agent; or (2) The rendering of treatment to a patient within this state by a physician located outside this state as a result of transmission of individual patient data by electronic or other means from within this state to such physician or physician's agent. Mo. Rev. Stat. § 334.010(2).
Montana	Mont. Code §§ 37-3-102((12), (13).	**Full License Required**	"Telemedicine" means the practice of medicine using interactive electronic communications, information technology, or other means between a licensee in one location and a patient in another location with or without an intervening health care provider. Telemedicine typically involves the application of secure videoconferencing or store-and-forward technology . . . . The term does not mean an audio-only telephone conversation, an e-mail or instant messaging conversation, or a message sent by facsimile transmission. Mont. Code § 37-3-102(13).

Table 1.1: Applicability of State Medical Licensure Requirements to Interstate Telemedicine			
Nebraska	Neb. Rev. Stat. §§ 38-121, 38-2024.	**Full License Required**	The . . . class of persons [who] shall be deemed to be engaged in the practice of medicine and surgery [includes] [p]ersons who are physically located in another state but who, through the use of any medium, including an electronic medium, perform for compensation any service which constitutes the healing arts that would affect the diagnosis or treatment of an individual located in this state. Neb. Rev. Stat. § 38-2024(7).
Nevada	Nev. Rev. Stat. §§ 630.020(3), 630.049, 630.160(1), 630.261(1)(e).	**Full or Special Purpose License Required**	"Practice of medicine" includes "[t]o perform any of the acts described in subsections 1 and 2 [concerning diagnosis, treatment, correction, prevention, prescription, etc.] by using equipment that transfers information concerning the medical condition of the patient electronically, telephonically or by fiber optics, including, without limitation, through telehealth, from within or outside this State or the United States." Nev. Rev. Stat. § 630.020(3) *see also id.* § 630.261(1)(e).
New Hampshire	N.H. Rev. Stat. § 329:1-d, 329:24.	**Full License Required**	"Telemedicine" means the use of audio, video, or other electronic media for the purpose of diagnosis consultation, or treatment. "Telemedicine" shall not include the use of audio-only telephone or facsimile. N.H. Rev. Stat. § 329:1-d(I).
New Jersey	N.J. Rev. Stat. §§ 45:9-5.1, 45:9-6.	**Telemedicine Not Directly Addressed**	
New Mexico	N.M. Stat. §§ 61-6-6(K), 61-6-11.1, 61-6-20; N.M. Admin. Code §§ 16.10.2.7(K), 16.10.2.11.	**Full or Special Purpose License Required**	"[T]he practice of medicine across state lines" means: (1) the rendering of a written or otherwise documented medical opinion concerning diagnosis or treatment of a patient within this state by a physician located outside this state as a result of transmission of individual patient data by electronic, telephonic or other means from within this state to the physician or the physician's agent; or (2) the rendering of treatment to a patient within this state by a physician located outside this state as a result of transmission of individual patient data by electronic, telephonic or other means from within this state to the physician or the physician's agent[.] N.M. Stat. § 61-6-6(K).
New York	N.Y. Educ. Law §§ 6521, 6522.	**Telemedicine Not Directly Addressed**	
North Carolina	N.C. Gen. Stat. § 90-18(a).	**Telemedicine Not Directly Addressed**	
North Dakota	N.D. Cent. Code § 43-17-01(3).	**Telemedicine Not Directly Addressed**	
Ohio	Ohio Rev. Code §§ 4731.296, 4731.34(A)(3), 4731.41.	**Full or Special Purpose Licensed Required**	"[T]he practice of telemedicine" means the practice of medicine in this state through the use of any communication, including oral, written, or electronic communication, by a physician located outside this state. Ohio Rev. Code § 4731.296(A).

Table 1.1: Applicability of State Medical Licensure Requirements to Interstate Telemedicine			
Oklahoma	Okla. Stat. §§ 59-491, 59-492(C)(3)(b).	**Full License Required**	The definition of the practice of medicine and surgery shall include, but is not limited to . . . performance by a person outside of this state, through an ongoing regular arrangement, of diagnostic or treatment services, including but not limited to, stroke prevention and treatment, through electronic communications for any patient whose condition is being diagnosed or treated within this state. 59 Okla. Stat. § 492(C)(3)(b).
Oregon	Or. Rev. Stat. §§ 677.080, 677.135, 677.137, 677.139.	**Full or Special Purpose License Required**	"[T]he practice of medicine across state lines" means: (1) The rendering directly to a person of a written or otherwise documented medical opinion concerning the diagnosis or treatment of that person located within this state for the purpose of patient care by a physician located outside this state as a result of the transmission of individual patient data by electronic or other means from within this state to that physician or the physician's agent; or (2) The rendering of medical treatment directly to a person located within this state by a physician located outside this state as a result of the outward transmission of individual patient data by electronic or other means from within this state to that physician or the physician's agent. Or. Rev. Stat. § 677.135.
Pennsylvania	63 Pa. Stat. § 422.10.	**Telemedicine Not Directly Addressed**	
Rhode Island	R.I. Gen. Laws §§ 5-37-1(15), 5-37-2(a), 5-37-12.	**Telemedicine Not Directly Addressed**	
South Carolina	S.C. Code § 40-47-20(36), 40-47-30.	**Full License Required**	"Practice of medicine" [includes] rendering a written or otherwise documented medical opinion concerning the diagnosis or treatment of a patient within this State by a physician located outside the State as a result of transmission of individual patient data by electronic or other means from within a state to such physician or his or her agent. S.C. Code § 40-47-20(36)(e).
South Dakota	S.D. Codified Laws §§ 36-4-8, 36-4-9, 36-4-41.	**Full License Required**	Any nonresident or osteopath who, while located outside this state, provides diagnostic or treatment services through electronic means to a patient located in this state under a contract with a health care provider licensed under Title 36, a clinic located in this state that provides health services, a health maintenance organization, a preferred provider organization, or a health care facility licensed under chapter 34-12, is engaged in the practice of medicine or osteopathy in this state. S.D. Codified Laws § 36-4-41.

Table 1.1: Applicability of State Medical Licensure Requirements to Interstate Telemedicine			
Tennessee	Tenn. Code §§ 63-6-201, 63-6-204, 63-6-231, 63-6-209(b), 63-6-214(b)(2); Tenn. Comp. R. & Reg. § 0880-2-.16.	**Full or Special Purpose License Required**	Telemedicine is the practice of medicine using electronic communication, information technology or other means, between a licensee in one location and a patient in another location. Telemedicine is not an audio only telephone conversation, email/instant messaging conversation or fax. It typically involves the application of secure video conferencing or store-and-forward to provide or support health care delivery by replicating the interaction of a traditional encounter between a provider and a patient. Tenn. Comp. R. & Reg. § 0880-02-.16(1)(g).
Texas	Tex. Occ. Code §§ 151.056, 155.001; Tex. Admin. Code § 172.12.	**Full or Special Purpose License Required**	A person who is physically located in another jurisdiction but who, through the use of any medium, including an electronic medium, performs an act that is part of a patient care service initiated in this state, including the taking of an x-ray examination or the preparation of pathological material for examination, and that would affect the diagnosis or treatment of the patient, is considered to be engaged in the practice of medicine in this state and is subject to appropriate regulation by the board. Tex. Occ. Code § 151.056(a).
Utah	Utah Code §§ 58-67-301, 58-67-102(12)(a).	**Full License Required**	"Practice of medicine" includes "to diagnose, treat, correct, administer anesthesia, or prescribe for any human disease, ailment, injury, infirmity, deformity, pain or other condition, physical or mental, real or imaginary, including to perform cosmetic medical procedures, or to attempt to do so, by any means or instrumentality, and by an individual in Utah or outside the state upon or for any human within the state." Utah Code § 58-67-102(12)(a).
Vermont	26 Vt. Stat. §§ 1311(1), 1314(a).	**Full License Required**	"Practice of medicine" includes "rendering a written or otherwise documented medical opinion concerning the diagnosis or treatment of a patient or the actual rendering of treatment to a patient within the State by a physician located outside the State as a result of the transmission of individual patient data by electronic or other means from within the State to the physician or his or her agent." 26 Vt. Stat. § 1311(1)(F).
Virginia	Va. Code §§ 54.1-2900, 2902, 2903, 2929.	**Telemedicine Not Directly Addressed**	
Washington	Wash. Rev. Code §§ 18.71.011, 18.71.021.	**Telemedicine Not Directly Addressed**	

Table 1.1: Applicability of State Medical Licensure Requirements to Interstate Telemedicine			
West Virginia	W. Va. Code §§ 30-3-13, 30-3-13a.	**Full License Required**	[T]he "practice of telemedicine" means the practice of medicine using communication tools such as electronic communication, information technology or other means of interaction between a licensed health care professional in one location and a patient in another location, with or without an intervening health care provider, and typically involves secure real time audio/video conferencing or similar secure audio/video services, remote monitoring, interactive video and store and forward digital image or health data technology to provide or support health care delivery by replicating the interaction of a traditional in person encounter between a provider and a patient. The practice of telemedicine occurs in this state when the patient receiving health care services through a telemedicine encounter is physically located in this state. W. Va. Code § 30-3-13(b); *see also id.* § 30-3-13a(a), (b).
Wisconsin	Wis. Stat. §§ 448.01(9), 448.03(1).	**Telemedicine Not Directly Addressed**	
Wyoming	Wyo. Stat. §§ 33-26-102(a)(xi), (xxix), 33-26-202(b)(xix), 33-26-301(a); Wyo. Bd. Med. R. ch.1, §§ 3(aaa), 4(e).	**Full License Required**	"Telemedicine" means the practice of medicine by electronic communication or other means from a physician in a location to a patient in another location, with or without an intervening health care provider. Wyo. Stat. § 33-26-102(a)(xxix).

Table 1.2 Physician-to-Physician Consultation Exceptions from Licensure Requirements

Table 1.2: Physician-to-Physician Consultation Exceptions from Licensure Requirements			
Unqualified	**Expressly Conditioned on Nature of Consultation**	**Expressly Conditioned on Frequency of Consultation**	**Expressly Conditioned on Nature and Frequency of Consultation**
Alabama			
	This definition [of the practice of medicine or osteopathy across state lines] is not intended to include an informal consultation between a licensed physician located in this state and a physician located outside this state provided that the consultation is conducted without compensation to or the expectation of compensation to either physician and does not result in the formal rendering of a written or otherwise documented medical opinion concerning the diagnosis or treatment of a patient by the physician located outside the state. Ala. Code § 34-24-501(a)(3).		A physician who engages in the practice of medicine or osteopathy across state lines on an irregular or infrequent basis is not subject to the provisions of this article [concerning licensing of such practice across state lines]. The 'irregular or infrequent' practice of medicine across state lines is deemed to occur if such practice occurs less than 10 times in a calendar year or involves fewer than 10 patients in a calendar year or comprises less than one percent of the physician's diagnostic or therapeutic practice. Ala. Code § 34-24-505(b).
Alaska			
This chapter [concerning medical licensing] does not apply to . . . a physician or osteopath, who is not a resident of this state, who is asked by a physician or osteopath licensed in this state to help in the diagnosis or treatment of a case. Alaska Stat. 08.64.370(2).			

Table 1.2: Physician-to-Physician Consultation Exceptions from Licensure Requirements			
Unqualified	**Expressly Conditioned on Nature of Consultation**	**Expressly Conditioned on Frequency of Consultation**	**Expressly Conditioned on Nature and Frequency of Consultation**
Arizona			
		This article [concerning medical licensure] does not apply to . . . [a] doctor of medicine residing in another jurisdiction who is authorized to practice medicine in that jurisdiction, if the doctor engages in actual single or infrequent consultation with a doctor of medicine licensed in this state and if the consultation regards a specific patient or patients. Ariz. Rev. Stat. § 32-1421(B)(1).	
Arkansas			
			This section [describing out-of-state physicians engaged in the practice of medicine in Arkansas] does not apply to . . . [t]he acts of a medical specialist located in another jurisdiction who provides only episodic consultation services. Ark. Code § 17-95-206(1).
California			
	Nothing in this chapter [concerning medicine] applies to any practitioner located outside this state, when in actual consultation, whether within this state or across state lines, with a licensed practitioner of this state. This practitioner shall not open an office, appoint a place to meet patients, receive calls from patients within the limits of this state, give orders, or have ultimate authority over the care or primary diagnosis of a patient who is located within this state. Cal. Bus. & Prof. Code § 2060.		

Table 1.2: Physician-to-Physician Consultation Exceptions from Licensure Requirements			
Unqualified	**Expressly Conditioned on Nature of Consultation**	**Expressly Conditioned on Frequency of Consultation**	**Expressly Conditioned on Nature and Frequency of Consultation**
Colorado			
			A person may engage in, and shall not be required to obtain a license or a physician training license under this article [concerning medical practice] with respect to . . . [t]he occasional rendering of services in this state by a physician if the physician: (I) Is licensed and lawfully practicing medicine in another state or territory of the United States without restrictions or conditions on the physician's license; (II) Does not have any established or regularly used medical staff membership or clinical privileges in this state; (III) Is not party to any contract, agreement, or understanding to provide services in this state on a regular or routine basis; (IV) Does not maintain an office or other place for the rendering of such services; (V) Has medical liability insurance coverage in the amounts required pursuant to section 13-64-302, C.R.S., for the services rendered in this state; and (VI) Limits the services provided in this state to an occasional case or consultation[.] Colo. Rev. Stat. § 12-36-106(3)(b).

Table 1.2: Physician-to-Physician Consultation Exceptions from Licensure Requirements			
Unqualified	**Expressly Conditioned on Nature of Consultation**	**Expressly Conditioned on Frequency of Consultation**	**Expressly Conditioned on Nature and Frequency of Consultation**
Connecticut			
		The provisions of subsection (a) of this section [concerning licensure] shall not apply to a nonresident physician who, while located outside this state, consults . . . on an irregular basis with a physician licensed by section 20-10 who is located in this state. Conn. Gen. Stat. § 20-9(d).	
Delaware			
This chapter [the Medical Practice Act] does not prevent a person who is certified, licensed, or otherwise authorized to practice medicine in another state or in a foreign country from engaging in a consultation with a person certified and registered to practice medicine in this State. 24 Del. Code § 1727.			Consultation may be done telephonically, electronically or in person. Consultation shall ordinarily consist of a history and physical examination, review of records and imaging pathology or similar studies. Consultation includes providing opinions and recommendations. An active Delaware certificate is required of any out of state physician who comes into Delaware to perform a consultation more than twelve (12) times per year. A physician who comes into Delaware to perform consultations must be actively licensed in another State or country on a full and unrestricted basis. 24 Del. Admin Code § 1700-6.0

Table 1.2: Physician-to-Physician Consultation Exceptions from Licensure Requirements

Unqualified	Expressly Conditioned on Nature of Consultation	Expressly Conditioned on Frequency of Consultation	Expressly Conditioned on Nature and Frequency of Consultation
District of Columbia			
The provisions of this chapter [concerning health occupation boards] prohibiting the practice of a health occupation without a District of Columbia license, registration, or certification shall not apply . . . [t]o an individual, licensed, registered, or certified to practice a health occupation in a state, who is providing care to an individual . . . or group for a limited period of time, or who is called from a state in professional consultation by or on behalf of a specific patient . . . or client to visit, examine, treat, or provide advice regarding the specific patient . . . or client in the District, or to give a demonstration of a procedure or clinic in the District; provided, that the individual engages in the provision of care, consultation, demonstration, or clinic in affiliation with a comparable health professional licensed, registered, or certified pursuant to this chapter. D.C. Code § 3-1205.02(a)(3).			
Florida			
[Various licensing] provisions . . . shall have no application to . . . [a]ny physician lawfully licensed in another state or territory . . . when meeting duly licensed physicians of this state in consultation. Fla. Stat. § 458.303(1)(b).			

Table 1.2: Physician-to-Physician Consultation Exceptions from Licensure Requirements			
Unqualified	**Expressly Conditioned on Nature of Consultation**	**Expressly Conditioned on Frequency of Consultation**	**Expressly Conditioned on Nature and Frequency of Consultation**
Georgia			
		This Code section [subjecting out-of-state telemedicine providers to Georgia licensure requirements] shall not apply to . . . the acts of a doctor of medicine or doctor of osteopathic medicine located in another state . . . who: (A) Provides consultation services at the request of a physician licensed in this state; and (B) Provides such services on an occasional rather than on a regular or routine basis. Ga. Code § 43-34-31(b)(1).	
Hawaii			
	Nothing [in this section requiring licensure] shall . . . [a]pply to any practitioner of medicine and surgery from another state when in actual consultation, including in-person, mail, electronic, telephonic, fiber-optic, or other telehealth consultation with a licensed physician or osteopathic physician of this State, if the physician or osteopathic physician from another state at the time of consultation is licensed to practice in the state in which the physician or osteopathic physician resides;		

Table 1.2: Physician-to-Physician Consultation Exceptions from Licensure Requirements			
Unqualified	**Expressly Conditioned on Nature of Consultation**	**Expressly Conditioned on Frequency of Consultation**	**Expressly Conditioned on Nature and Frequency of Consultation**
Hawaii, continued			
	provided that: (A) The physician or osteopathic physician from another state shall not open an office, or appoint a place to meet patients in this State, or receive calls within the limits of the State for the provision of care for a patient who is located in this State; (B) The licensed physician or osteopathic physician of this State retains control and remains responsible for the provision of care for the patient who is located in this State; and (C) The laws and rules relating to contagious diseases are not violated[.] Haw. Rev. Stat. § 453-2(b)(4).		
Idaho			
	"[P]ersons" who, "though not holding a license to practice medicine in this state, may engage in activities included in the practice of medicine" include "[a] person residing in another state or country and authorized to practice medicine there, who is called in consultation by a person licensed in this state to practice medicine . . . , so long as he does not open an office or appoint a place to meet patients or receive calls in this state." Idaho Code § 54-1804(1)(b).		

Table 1.2: Physician-to-Physician Consultation Exceptions from Licensure Requirements			
Unqualified	**Expressly Conditioned on Nature of Consultation**	**Expressly Conditioned on Frequency of Consultation**	**Expressly Conditioned on Nature and Frequency of Consultation**
Illinois			
	"Telemedicine" does not include . . . a second opinion provided to a person licensed under this Act. 225 Ill. Comp. Stat. § 60/ 49.5(c)(2).		
Indiana			
This article [concerning physicians], as it relates to the unlawful or unauthorized practice of medicine or osteopathic medicine, does not apply to . . . [a]n individual who is not a licensee who resides in another state or country and is authorized to practice medicine or osteopathic medicine there, who is called in for consultation by an individual licensed to practice medicine or osteopathic medicine in Indiana. Ind. Code § 25-22.5-1-2.	[A] nonresident physician who is located outside Indiana does not practice medicine or osteopathy in Indiana by providing a second opinion to a licensee . . . . Ind. Code § 25-22.5-1-1.1(a)(4).		
Iowa			
			Section 148.1 [describing persons engaged in the practice of medicine] shall not be construed to include . . . physicians and surgeons or osteopathic physicians licensed in another state, when incidentally called into this state in consultation with a physician and surgeon or osteopathic physician and surgeon licensed in this state," Iowa Code § 148.2(5),

Table 1.2: Physician-to-Physician Consultation Exceptions from Licensure Requirements			
Unqualified	**Expressly Conditioned on Nature of Consultation**	**Expressly Conditioned on Frequency of Consultation**	**Expressly Conditioned on Nature and Frequency of Consultation**
Iowa, continued			
			which "means all of the following shall be true: (1) The consulting physician shall be involved in the care of patients in Iowa only at the request of an Iowa-licensed physician. (2) The consulting physician has a license in good standing in another United States jurisdiction. (3) The consulting physician provides expertise and acts in an advisory capacity to an Iowa-licensed physician. The consulting physician may examine the patient and advise an Iowa-licensed physician as to the care that should be provided, but the consulting physician may not personally perform procedures, write orders, or prescribe for the patient. (4) The consulting physician practices in Iowa for a period not greater than 10 consecutive days and not more than 20 total days in any calendar year. Any portion of a day counts as one day. (5) The Iowa-licensed physician requesting the consultation retains the primary responsibility for the management of the patient's care," Iowa Admin. Code § 653-9.1.

Table 1.2: Physician-to-Physician Consultation Exceptions from Licensure Requirements			
Unqualified	**Expressly Conditioned on Nature of Consultation**	**Expressly Conditioned on Frequency of Consultation**	**Expressly Conditioned on Nature and Frequency of Consultation**
Kansas			
The practice of the healing arts shall not be construed to include . . . [p]ractitioners of the healing arts licensed in another state when and while incidentally called into this state in consultation with practitioners licensed in this state. Kan. Stat. § 65-2872(j).			The practice of the healing arts shall not be construed to include . . . [p]ractitioners of the healing arts licensed under the laws of another state who do not open an office or maintain or appoint a place to regularly meet patients or to receive calls within this state, but who order services which are performed in this state in accordance with rules and regulations of the board. Kan. Stat. § 65-2872(r).
Kentucky			
		The provisions of subsection (1) of this section [prohibiting the practice of medicine or osteopathy without a license] shall not apply to . . . [p]ersons who, being nonresidents of Kentucky and lawfully licensed to practice medicine or osteopathy in their states of actual residence, infrequently engage in the practice of medicine or osteopathy within this state, when called to see or attend particular patients in consultation and association with a physician licensed pursuant to this chapter. Ky. Rev. Stat. § 311.560(2)(b)(1).	

Table 1.2: Physician-to-Physician Consultation Exceptions from Licensure Requirements			
Unqualified	**Expressly Conditioned on Nature of Consultation**	**Expressly Conditioned on Frequency of Consultation**	**Expressly Conditioned on Nature and Frequency of Consultation**
Louisiana			
	"The . . . activities . . . exempt from the requirements of this Chapter [governing the use of telemedicine by physicians licensed to practice medicine in this state and those who hold a telemedicine permit issued by the board to practice medicine in this state via telemedicine]" include "a true consultation, e.g., an informal consultation or second opinion, provided by an individual licensed to practice medicine in a state other than Louisiana, provided that the Louisiana physician receiving the opinion is personally responsible to the patient for the primary diagnosis and any testing and treatment provided." 46 La. Admin. Code § 7515(A)(1).		
Maine			
			Consultation shall be considered to occur when a physician not licensed in the State of Maine reviews records or interviews or examines a patient in any way, and provide a professional opinion or recommendation to a physician licensed in the State of Maine who is the physician of record for the patient being diagnosed or treated. Such consultant must be fully licensed in another state. A non-resident physician does not need a license in this State if he/she consults on an irregular basis with a physician or physicians licensed in this State. 02-373-1 Code Me. R. § 2(4)(B).

Table 1.2: Physician-to-Physician Consultation Exceptions from Licensure Requirements			
Unqualified	**Expressly Conditioned on Nature of Consultation**	**Expressly Conditioned on Frequency of Consultation**	**Expressly Conditioned on Nature and Frequency of Consultation**
Maryland			
	[I]ndividuals [who] may practice medicine without a license [include a] physician licensed by and residing in another jurisdiction, if the physician . . . [i]s engaged in consultation with a physician licensed in the State about a particular patient and does not direct patient care. Md. Code, Health Occ. § 14-302(a)(2)(i).		
Massachusetts			
Certain licensing and registration requirements "shall not apply . . . to a physician or surgeon resident in another state who is a legal practitioner therein, when in actual consultation with a legal practitioner of the commonwealth. Mass. Gen. Laws ch. 112, § 7.			
Michigan			
	Among the "individuals [who] are not required to have a license issued under this article for practice of a health profession in this state" is "[a]n individual who resides in another state or country and is authorized to practice a health profession in that state or country who, in an exceptional circumstance, is called in for consultation or treatment by a health professional in this state." Mich. Comp. Laws § 333.16171(e).		

Table 1.2: Physician-to-Physician Consultation Exceptions from Licensure Requirements			
Unqualified	**Expressly Conditioned on Nature of Consultation**	**Expressly Conditioned on Frequency of Consultation**	**Expressly Conditioned on Nature and Frequency of Consultation**
Minnesota			
	A physician who is not licensed to practice medicine in this state, but who holds a valid license to practice medicine in another state or jurisdiction, and who provides interstate telemedicine services to a patient located in this state is not subject to the registration requirement of subdivision 1, paragraph (a), clause (4), if . . . the physician provides interstate telemedicine services in this state in consultation with a physician licensed in this state and the Minnesota physician retains ultimate authority over the diagnosis and care of the patient. Minn. Stat. § 147.032-2(3).		A physician who is not licensed to practice medicine in this state, but who holds a valid license to practice medicine in another state or jurisdiction, and who provides interstate telemedicine services to a patient located in this state is not subject to the registration requirement of subdivision 1, paragraph (a), clause (4), if . . . the services are provided on an irregular or infrequent basis. For the purposes of this section, a person provides services on an irregular or infrequent basis if the person provides the services less than once a month or provides the services to fewer than ten patients annually. Minn. Stat. § 147.032-2(2).
Mississippi			
	The requirement of licensure . . . shall not be required where the evaluation, treatment and/or the medical opinion to be rendered by a physician outside this state (a) is requested by a physician duly licensed to practice medicine in this state, and (b) the physician who has requested such evaluation, treatment and/or medical opinion has already established a doctor/patient relationship with the patient to be evaluated and/or treated. Miss. Code § 73-25-34(3).		

Table 1.2: Physician-to-Physician Consultation Exceptions from Licensure Requirements			
Unqualified	**Expressly Conditioned on Nature of Consultation**	**Expressly Conditioned on Frequency of Consultation**	**Expressly Conditioned on Nature and Frequency of Consultation**
Missouri			
	A physician located outside of this state shall not be required to obtain a license when: (1) In consultation with a physician licensed to practice medicine in this state; and (2) The physician licensed in this state retains ultimate authority and responsibility for the diagnosis or diagnoses and treatment in the care of the patient located within this state . . . . Mo. Rev. Stat. § 334.010(3).		
Montana			
			This chapter [regarding medicine] does not prohibit or require a license with respect to . . . the rendering of services in this state by a physician lawfully practicing medicine in another state or territory. However, if the physician does not limit the services to an occasional case or if the physician has any established or regularly used hospital connections in this state or maintains or is provided with, for the physician's regular use, an office or other place for rending the services, the physician must possess a license to practice medicine in this state. Mont. Code § 37-3-103(1)(b).

Table 1.2: Physician-to-Physician Consultation Exceptions from Licensure Requirements			
Unqualified	**Expressly Conditioned on Nature of Consultation**	**Expressly Conditioned on Frequency of Consultation**	**Expressly Conditioned on Nature and Frequency of Consultation**
Nebraska			
	The . . . classes of persons [who] shall not be construed to be engaged in the unauthorized practice of medicine [include] [p]hysicians who are licensed in good standing to practice medicine under the laws of another state when incidentally called into this state or contacted via electronic or other medium for consultation with a physician licensed in this state. For purposes of this subdivision, consultation means evaluating the medical data of the patient as provided by the treating physician and rendering a recommendation to such treating physician as to the method of treatment or analysis of the data. The interpretation of a radiological image by a physician who specializes in radiology is not a consultation . . . . Neb. Rev. Stat. § 38-2025(6).		This chapter [regulating the medical profession] does not apply to . . . [p]hysicians who are called into this State, other than on a regular basis, for consultation with or assistance to a physician licensed in this State, and who are legally qualified to practice in the state where they reside. Nev. Rev. Stat. § 630.047(1)(b); *see also* Nev. Admin. Code § 630.225 (requiring Nevada-licensed physicians to notify Board if any unlicensed physician "comes into this State for consultation with or assistance to the physician licensed in this State").

Table 1.2: Physician-to-Physician Consultation Exceptions from Licensure Requirements			
Unqualified	**Expressly Conditioned on Nature of Consultation**	**Expressly Conditioned on Frequency of Consultation**	**Expressly Conditioned on Nature and Frequency of Consultation**
Nevada			
			The . . . classes of persons [who] shall not be construed to be engaged in the unauthorized practice of medicine [include] [p]hysicians who are licensed in good standing to practice medicine in another state but who, from such other state, order diagnostic or therapeutic services on an irregular or occasional basis, to be provided to an individual in this state, if such physicians do not maintain and are not furnished for regular use within this state any office or other place for the rendering of professional services or the receipt of calls . . . . Neb. Rev. Stat. § 38-2025(7).

Table 1.2: Physician-to-Physician Consultation Exceptions from Licensure Requirements			
Unqualified	**Expressly Conditioned on Nature of Consultation**	**Expressly Conditioned on Frequency of Consultation**	**Expressly Conditioned on Nature and Frequency of Consultation**
New Hampshire			
		This chapter [regulating physicians and surgeons] shall not apply . . . [t]o legally qualified physicians in other states or countries when called in consultation by an individual licensed to practice in the state who bears the responsibility for the patient's diagnosis and treatment. However, regular or frequent consultation by such an unlicensed person, as determined by the licensing board, shall constitute the practice of medicine without a license . . . . N.H. Rev. Stat. § 329:21(II).	
New Jersey			
			The prohibitory provisions of this chapter shall not apply to . . . [a] physician or surgeon of another state of the United States and duly authorized under the laws thereof to practice medicine or surgery therein, if such practitioner does not open an office or place for the practice of his profession in this State. N.J. Rev. Stat. § 45:9-21(c).

Table 1.2: Physician-to-Physician Consultation Exceptions from Licensure Requirements			
Unqualified	**Expressly Conditioned on Nature of Consultation**	**Expressly Conditioned on Frequency of Consultation**	**Expressly Conditioned on Nature and Frequency of Consultation**
New Mexico			
		The Medical Practice Act shall not apply to or affect . . . a physician licensed to practice under the laws of another state who acts as a consultant to a New Mexico-licensed physician on an irregular or infrequent basis, as defined by rule of the board. N.M. Stat. § 61-6-17(L). Exemptions from licensure requirements are defined in Section 61-6-17 of the Medical Practice Act and include a physician licensed to practice under the laws of another state who acts as a consultant to a New Mexico licensed physician on an irregular or infrequent basis not to exceed ten patients per year. N.M. Admin. Code § 16.10.2.11(E).	The Medical Practice Act shall not apply to or affect . . . a physician who engages in the informal practice of medicine across state lines without compensation or expectation of compensation; provided that the practice of medicine across state lines conducted within the parameters of a contractual relationship shall not be considered informal and is subject to licensure and rule by the board. N.M. Stat. § 61-6-17(M).
New York			
"The following persons under the following limitations may practice medicine within the state without a license," including "[a]ny physician who is licensed in another state or country and who is meeting a physician licensed in this state, for purposes of consultation, provided such practice is limited to such consultation." N.Y. Educ. Law § 6526(3).			

Table 1.2: Physician-to-Physician Consultation Exceptions from Licensure Requirements			
Unqualified	**Expressly Conditioned on Nature of Consultation**	**Expressly Conditioned on Frequency of Consultation**	**Expressly Conditioned on Nature and Frequency of Consultation**
North Carolina			
		"The following shall not constitute practicing medicine or surgery as defined in this Article," including "[t]he practice of medicine or surgery by any nonregistered reputable physician or surgeon who comes into this State, either in person or by use of any electronic or other mediums, on an irregular basis, to consult with a resident registered physician . . . . This proviso shall not apply to physicians resident in a neighboring state and regularly practicing in this State. N.C. Gen. Stat. § 90-18(c)(11).	
North Dakota			
			Notwithstanding anything in this chapter [concerning physicians and surgeons] to the contrary, any physician who is the holder of a permanent, unrestricted license to practice medicine or osteopathy in any state or territory of the United States, the District of Columbia, or a province of Canada may practice medicine or osteopathy in this state without first obtaining a license from the North Dakota board of medicine under one or more of the following circumstances," including "[t]o provide one-time consultation . . . for a period of not more than twenty-four hours." N.D. Cent. Code § 43-17-02.3(3).

Table 1.2: Physician-to-Physician Consultation Exceptions from Licensure Requirements			
Unqualified	**Expressly Conditioned on Nature of Consultation**	**Expressly Conditioned on Frequency of Consultation**	**Expressly Conditioned on Nature and Frequency of Consultation**
Ohio			
	Sections 4731.01 to 4731.47 of the Revised Code shall not apply to . . . [a] physician or surgeon in another state or territory who is a legal practitioner of medicine or surgery therein when providing consultation to an individual holding a certificate to practice issued under this chapter who is responsible for the examination, diagnosis, and treatment of the patient who is the subject of the consultation, if . . . [t]he physician or surgeon provides the consultation without compensation of any kind, direct or indirect, for the consultation. Ohio Rev. Code § 4731.36(A)(3)(b).	Sections 4731.01 to 4731.47 of the Revised Code shall not apply to . . . [a] physician or surgeon in another state or territory who is a legal practitioner of medicine or surgery therein when providing consultation to an individual holding a certificate to practice issued under this chapter who is responsible for the examination, diagnosis, and treatment of the patient who is the subject of the consultation, if . . . [t]he physician or surgeon does not provide consultation in this state on a regular or frequent basis. Ohio Rev. Code § 4731.36(A)(3)(a).	
Oklahoma			
	The practice of medicine and surgery . . . shall not include . . . [a]ny person who is licensed to practice medicine and surgery in another state or territory of the United States whose sole purpose and activity is limited to brief actual consultation with a specific physician who is licensed to practice medicine and surgery by the Board, other than a person with a special or restricted license. 59 Okla. Stat. § 492(D).		

Table 1.2: Physician-to-Physician Consultation Exceptions from Licensure Requirements			
Unqualified	**Expressly Conditioned on Nature of Consultation**	**Expressly Conditioned on Frequency of Consultation**	**Expressly Conditioned on Nature and Frequency of Consultation**
Oregon			
	ORS 677.135 to 677.141 [concerning practice of medicine across state lines] do not apply to a licensed physician located outside this state who: (a) Consults with another physician licensed to practice medicine in this state; and (b) Does not undertake the primary responsibility for diagnosing or rendering treatment to a patient within this state. Or. Rev. Stat. § 677.137(3).		
Pennsylvania			
A person authorized to practice medicine or surgery or osteopathy without restriction by any other state may, upon request by a medical doctor, provide consultation to the medical doctor regarding the treatment of a patient under the care of the medical doctor. 63 Pa. Stat. § 422.16.			

Table 1.2: Physician-to-Physician Consultation Exceptions from Licensure Requirements			
Unqualified	**Expressly Conditioned on Nature of Consultation**	**Expressly Conditioned on Frequency of Consultation**	**Expressly Conditioned on Nature and Frequency of Consultation**
Rhode Island			
			A physician who is licensed to practice medicine in another state or states, but not in this state, and who is in good standing in such state or states, may exercise the privilege to practice medicine for a patient located in this state [if] [t]he physician, whether or not physically present in this state, is being consulted on a singular occasion by a physician licensed in this state . . . for a period not to exceed seven (7) days. Under no circumstance may a physician who is not present in this state provide consultation to a patient in this state who does not have a physician patient relationship with that physician unless that patient is in the physical presence of a physician licensed in this state. R.I. Gen. Laws § 5-37-16.2(a)(3).
South Carolina			
Nothing in this article [requiring licensure] may be construed to . . . prohibit a physician from practicing in actual consultation with a physician licensed in this State concerning an opinion for the South Carolina physician's consideration in managing the care or treatment of a patient in this State. S.C. Code § 40-47-30(A)(10).			

Table 1.2: Physician-to-Physician Consultation Exceptions from Licensure Requirements			
Unqualified	**Expressly Conditioned on Nature of Consultation**	**Expressly Conditioned on Frequency of Consultation**	**Expressly Conditioned on Nature and Frequency of Consultation**
South Dakota			
Nothing contained in this chapter [concerning practitioners of healing arts in general] shall be construed to apply to any licensed person practicing any of the healing arts outside of this state when in actual consultation with a licensed practitioner of the healing arts in this state. S.D. Codified Laws § 36-2-9; *see also id.* § 36-4-41.			
Tennessee			
This chapter [concerning medicine and surgery] shall not apply . . . to any registered physician or surgeon of other states when called in consultation by a registered physician of this state . . . . Tenn. Code § 63-6-204(a)(3); *see also* Tenn. Comp. R. & Reg. § 0880-02-.16(4).			
Texas			
	The . . . activities . . . exempt from the requirements of an out-of-state telemedicine license" include "consultation services provided by a medical specialist located in another jurisdiction who provides such consultation services on request to a person licensed in this state Tex. Admin. Code § 172.12(f)(1); *see also* Tex. Occ. Code § 151.056(b)(1).		The . . . activities . . . exempt from the requirements of an out-of-state telemedicine license" include "informal consultation performed by a physician outside the context of a contractual relationship and on an irregular or infrequent basis without the expectation or exchange of direct or indirect compensation. Tex. Admin. Code § 172.12(f)(4).

Table 1.2: Physician-to-Physician Consultation Exceptions from Licensure Requirements			
Unqualified	**Expressly Conditioned on Nature of Consultation**	**Expressly Conditioned on Frequency of Consultation**	**Expressly Conditioned on Nature and Frequency of Consultation**
Utah			
Except as otherwise provided by statute or rule, the following individuals may engage in the practice of their occupation or profession, subject to the stated circumstances and limitations, without being licensed under this title," including "an individual residing in another state and licensed to practice a regulated occupation or profession in that state, who is called in for a consultation by an individual licensed in this state, and the services are limited to that consultation. Utah Code § 58-1-307(1)(d).			
Vermont			
The provisions of this chapter [concerning medicine] shall not apply to . . . a nonresident physician coming into this State to consult or using telecommunications to consult with a duly licensed practitioner herein. 26 Vt. Stat. § 1313(a)(3).			
Virginia			
The provisions of this chapter [concerning medicine and other healing arts] shall not prevent or prohibit . . . [a]ny legally qualified out-of-state or foreign practitioner from meeting in consultation with legally licensed practitioners in this Commonwealth. Va. Code § 54.1-2901(15).			

Table 1.2: Physician-to-Physician Consultation Exceptions from Licensure Requirements			
Unqualified	**Expressly Conditioned on Nature of Consultation**	**Expressly Conditioned on Frequency of Consultation**	**Expressly Conditioned on Nature and Frequency of Consultation**
Washington			
			Nothing in this chapter shall be . . . construed to prohibit . . . [t]he practice of medicine by any practitioner licensed by another state or territory in which he or she resides, provided that such practitioner shall not open an office or appoint a place of meeting patients or receiving calls within this state. Wash. Rev. Code § 18.71.030(6).
West Virginia			
	This section [requiring licensure for telemedicine] does not apply to . . . [a]n informal consultation or second opinion, at the request of a physician or podiatrist who is licensed to practice medicine or podiatry in this state, provided that the physician or podiatrist requesting the opinion retains authority and responsibility for the patient's care . . . . W. Va. Code § 30-3-13a(b)(3)(A).		
Wisconsin			
Nothing in this subchapter [concerning licensure] shall be construed either to prohibit, or to require, a license or certificate under this subchapter for . . . [a]ctual consultation or demonstration by licensed physicians . . . of other states or countries with licensed physicians . . . of this state. Wis. Stat. § 448.03(2)(d).			

Table 1.2: Physician-to-Physician Consultation Exceptions from Licensure Requirements			
Unqualified	**Expressly Conditioned on Nature of Consultation**	**Expressly Conditioned on Frequency of Consultation**	**Expressly Conditioned on Nature and Frequency of Consultation**
Wyoming			
		Physicians residing in and currently licensed in good standing to practice medicine in another state or country brought into this state for consultation by a physician licensed to practice medicine in this state may practice medicine without first obtaining a Wyoming license for a total of not more than twelve (12) days in any fifty-two (52) week period and, therefore, are exempt from the licensure requirements of these rules and W.S. 33-26-103(a)(iv). Consults of longer duration or greater frequency require written advance approval of a majority of the Board officers. To qualify a consulting physician for the exemption from licensure, the physician licensed to practice medicine in this state shall notify the board, on a form published or approved by the Board, of the consultation in advance of the consulting physician practicing medicine in this state. For purposes of this subsection, the term "brought into this state" means having patient contact and establishing a physician-patient relationship, either by the physician's physical presence with the patient or through telemedicine. Wyo. Bd. Med. R. ch.1, § 7(a); see also Wyo. Stat. § 33-26-103(a)(iv).	

Chapter 2

Telehealth Regulatory Requirements

2.1 Introduction

Sometimes referred to as telehealth "practice standards," the rules governing where and how telehealth may be used to deliver care are largely determined at the state level. Federal laws create some legal and practical considerations for telehealth providers, including through limitations on the ability to prescribe controlled substances via telehealth under the Ryan Haight Act of 2008 and standards for Medicare reimbursement for telehealth services as discussed in Chapter 3. In addition, certain other federal laws governing health care providers more generally may be implicated in new or different ways through the use of telehealth as discussed in Chapter 1. However, because medical, nursing, and other health care professionals are regulated at the state level, the use of telehealth in the delivery of medical care and treatment is likewise primarily a state issue.

A flurry of legislative activity in recent years, together with increased focus on the use of telehealth by state medical boards, has resulted in some statutory or regulatory requirements governing the use of telehealth in almost every state. These requirements are codified in a number of places, including through statutes and regulations governing the use of telehealth generally, pharmacy statutes and regulations restricting the ability of providers to prescribe and/or pharmacists to dispense, and regulations or policy statements issued by medical, nursing and other professional licensing boards with authority over the professional practice of their licensees.

While not every state has promulgated a comprehensive (or in some cases, internally consistent) set of standards for the use of telehealth, there are a number of core issues that states have either addressed or that may arise for providers navigating how to use telehealth in compliance with applicable state requirements, including:

- How is "telehealth" or "telemedicine" defined? (i.e., Will the particular use of technology at issue meet the applicable definition?)
- What kinds of providers can deliver care using telehealth? Is it just physicians, or can other categories of providers and/or allied health professionals provide telehealth services?
- Can a physician or other licensed professional supervise another provider remotely?
- Can a provider establish a provider-patient relationship through a telehealth encounter, or must the relationship be established in-person prior to using telehealth in the delivery of care?
- If the provider-patient relationship can be established through a telehealth encounter, what requirements must be met? (e.g., physical evaluation or examination, disclosure of provider credentials, validation of patient location)
- What level of visual and/or auditory access to the patient, if any, is required for a telehealth encounter? (e.g., "real-time" audio and video)
- What kind of diagnostic equipment or technology, if any, must be used in a telehealth encounter? (e.g., ability to take temperature, pulse or other vitals)
- Does the provider need to obtain written or verbal informed consent from a patient prior to

the use of telehealth?

- What sort of disclosures or arrangements does the provider need to make relating to emergency or follow-up care for a patient receiving telehealth services?

In some cases, states have also created, whether intentionally or by virtue of outdated statutes or regulations, additional or differing requirements that limit the ability of a provider to prescribe medication based on a telehealth encounter or impose restrictions on the circumstances under which a pharmacist may dispense medications that involve telehealth services. These requirements generally are codified in pharmacy statutes and regulations, but can also take the form of professional conduct rules embedded in statutes and regulations governing the practice of the applicable licensed profession.

This chapter provides an overview of some of the primary considerations and limitations of state regulatory frameworks that may impact telehealth providers. Because of the evolving nature of state-based telehealth requirements and industry practices as a whole, we recommend always checking the most current laws, regulations and other guidance promulgated within a particular state to determine the applicable requirements at any given time.

2.2 Telehealth Models

2.2.1 Telehealth Communication Platforms

Telehealth services come in various shapes and sizes. The Institute of Medicine put it well when, back in 1996, it described telemedicine as

> not a single technology or a discrete set of related technologies; it is, rather, a large and very heterogeneous collection of clinical practices, technologies and organizational arrangements. In addition, widespread adoption of effective telemedicine applications depends on a complex, broadly distributed technical and human infrastructure that is only partly in place and is being profoundly affected by rapid changes in health care, information and communications systems.[1]

Though this guidance was issued over two decades ago, the IOM's description still captures today's spectrum and variety of telehealth delivery models. The key variables within these models relate to the type of communication, those involved in the communication and the equipment and infrastructure used to create the communication.

Telehealth services may be provided through two primary categories of communication platforms: (1) synchronous communication, described as "real-time" communication, or (2) "asynchronous" communications, which is known more commonly as "store and forward." As further described below, which platform is permissible, and the standards that may apply to the use of a given platform vary among states. However, most states generally treat audio-only, fax, and email communications as being insufficient, on their own, to satisfy the definition of telehealth and/or applicable telehealth statutory or regulatory requirements.[2] Likewise, the Federation of State Medical Boards (FSMB), in its Model Policy for the Appropriate Use of Telemedicine Technologies (hereinafter FSMB Model Policy), states that telemedicine is "[g]enerally . . . not an audio-only, telephone conversation, email/instant messaging conversation, or fax. It typically involves the application of secure videoconferencing or store and forward technology to provide or support healthcare delivery . . . ."[3]

---

[1] Inst. of Med., Comm. on Evaluating Clinical Applications of Telemedicine, Telemedicine: A Guide to Assessing Telecommunications for Health Care (Marilyn J. Field, ed., 1996).

[2] *See, e.g.*, Fla. Admin. Code Ann. r. 64B15-14.0081(1), (9) (2016); La. Stat. Ann. § 37:1262 (2008); La. Admin. Code tit. 46:XLV, §§ 7503 (2017); Tenn. Code Ann. § 63-1-155 (2015).

[3] Fed. St. Med. Boards, Model Policy for the Appropriate Use of Telemedicine Technologies § 3 (2014).

2.2.1.1 Synchronous Communication

Synchronous communication enables a provider, consumer or patient at the originating site to engage in live/real-time interaction with a provider in a remote location. The remote provider is viewing and speaking with the patient at the same time the patient is viewing and speaking with the provider. The communication is most often via an audio and visual connection. In fact, a number of states permit the provision of telehealth *only* through a synchronous connection, or require the use of a synchronous connect in certain circumstances. For example, Delaware requires that, absent a prior in-person examination, a telemedicine consult must be performed using video-audio communications.[4]

Through synchronous communication, patients who want to "see" a provider can do so. Even if the patient does not want to or cannot travel, the patient still is able to have a "live" consultation. Synchronous communication is also the clear choice in urgent situations, such as consultations regarding impending strokes. In the inpatient setting, hospitals without neurologists on staff may arrange for a neurological consult via telemedicine much more quickly than an in-person consult. That being said, a telehealth practice standard is for providers to assess when the urgency of a situation should prevent the use of telehealth and patients should be referred to in-person providers, or even to the local emergency department.

2.2.1.2 Asynchronous

Asynchronous communication is also referred to as "store and forward" because information is collected from the patient at the originating site—whether the patient's home or health care facility or physician practice—and then sent, or "*forwarded*," to the provider at the distant site who will assess the information. Common examples of data collected in a store-and-forward model are x-ray or CT images, lab test results, or pre-recorded videos or photographic images of an afflicted body part, such as throat or ear, and perhaps the patient's description of any symptoms.

Professional organizations such as the American Medical Association (AMA) and the FSMB recognize both types of telemedicine technology platforms. In the past, some states excluded asynchronous platforms from their definitions of telehealth; however, the current trend is to take a more inclusive approach like the AMA and FSMB. For example, Arkansas recently repealed a law that expressly carved out asynchronous technology from its definition of telemedicine, and new Hawaii legislation includes all models and modalities discussed herein as well as m-health to define the more global category of telehealth.[5]

Asynchronous communication can provide valuable benefits and is most suitable when immediate feedback is not needed or not possible. In asynchronistic RPM models, data is collected for later review. For example, in the traditional non-telehealth setting, diagnostic tests are processed and interpreted with the results delivered to the interpreting provider. Similarly, in the telehealth setting, real-time communication is not necessary. Diagnostic tests may be performed and the results sent electronically to the receiving provider at a distant site in a form and format that allows a specialist to properly interpret the results. In fact, if the specialist is not otherwise readily available, the use of telehealth technology may expedite the process. Further, asynchronous models can often be less expensive than services provided in the traditional setting.

Some states expressly require that asynchronous telehealth technology meet current practice standards, have security measures in place and generally be able adequately to provide the health

---

[4] 24 Del. Code § 1769D(h).

[5] 2017 Ark. Laws Act 203 (S.B. 146); Haw. Rev. Stat. §§ 346-59.1, 457-17, 671-7, 431-10A-116.3, 432-1-601.5, 432D-23.5, 453-1.3, 453-2, 457-2, & 466J-6 (2017).

care service. Missouri has mandated the promulgation of regulations governing the use of asynchronous technology. Such regulations must: (1) establish appropriate standards for the use of asynchronous store-and-forward technology in the practice of telehealth; (2) provide for certification of agencies offering asynchronous store-and-forward technology in the practice of telehealth; (3) establish timelines for completion of a consultation and the communication of the results or asking for additional information; (4) determine the length of time digital files of such asynchronous store-and-forward services are to be maintained; (5) address the security and privacy of such digital files; (6) address participant consent requirements for asynchronous store-and-forward services; and (7) address payment for services by providers and establish that consulting providers are not entitled to payment unless and until an opinion is rendered.[6]

2.2.2 Participant-Type Communication Models

2.2.2.1 Provider-to-Provider Models

Provider-to-provider communications are those in which a health care provider is at both ends of the communication, (i.e., at both the originating site with the patient and the distant site). One common use of the provider-to-provider model is to facilitate a remote specialist consult. In these scenarios, the present and treating provider at the originating site determines if additional consultation is required. The provider at the originating site could, for example, be the patient's primary care provider during an office visit, a nurse practitioner within an urgent care center or retail-based clinic, or a hospital's attending physician treating an inpatient. The remote consulting specialist or other providers renders the consult in the normal course, but via telemedicine.

Depending on the telemedicine arrangement, consultations may be requested and received on demand, and perhaps in minutes, or scheduled in advance. Telehealth consultation arrangements with remote providers also could require, as a term of the engagement, that the remote consulting provider respond to the consultation request within a certain time frame, particularly in the context of urgent care. For example, individuals seeking care at a retail clinic often do not have an ongoing relationship with the clinic. In clinic situations, individuals may seek quick assessments of their symptoms to determine whether further and more specialized medical care is required. A prompt consult is thus key to the success of this provider-to-provider model and one benefit over a traditional in-person consult.

While the on-demand characteristic is a draw of telehealth use for many, it is not always necessary. Telehealth consults scheduled in advance can be very helpful for the patient and the patient's treating (in-person) provider. For example, primary care providers in a rural area may recommend specialty consults for patient care; however, there are no applicable specialists in the area. In a provider-to-provider model, the primary care provider and patient can schedule a future telehealth appointment or consultation with the specialist, at which time the patient will participate from the primary care physician's office in the presence of his or her physician.

Provider-to-provider consultations do not always take place in the patient's presence, even in the case of in-person provider-to-provider consultations. For example, when an attending physician requires a neurological consult regarding a patient's MRI, the attending physician often determines the patient's presence is not necessary or perhaps advisable in his or her medical judgment. The attending physician consults with the neurologist in the absence of the patient and later conveys any information deemed necessary. The same can occur, and often more easily, via telehealth. And, with telehealth, the spectrum of consultant options can be exponentially increased.

Another benefit of provider-to-provider consultations, as discussed in Chapter 1, is the flexibility of licensing requirements.

---

[6] Mo. Rev. Stat. § 208.671 (2016).

2.2.2.2 Provider-to-Provider Extender

A provider-to-provider extender model involves a treating provider at the distant site and the patient in the company of an intervening ancillary health care provider, such as a registered nurse, at the originating site. The ancillary provider is often tasked with collecting information from the patient, such as vital signs or current symptoms of an ailment or condition, and acts as an extender of the distant site telehealth provider. The ancillary provider at the originating site communicates the data in real-time to the treating telehealth physician at the distant site through the telehealth communication connection. In these models, the ancillary provider also may have the ability to upload the patient's information into a database for the distant site treating provider's later review (i.e., "store and forward," as discussed below). Ancillary providers also are often used to assist with the patient's use of telemedicine equipment, such as cameras and scopes used to examine specific parts of the patient's body (e.g., throat, ears, eyes, wounds, skin irritations, etc.). Again, the data (i.e., images, videos, etc.) is either viewed in real-time or stored in an electronic platform for later review. Use of ancillary providers may occur not only in a facility or practice setting, but also when a patient receives telehealth services at home. In provider-to-provider extender models, relevant federal or state supervision requirements, as discussed in § 2.5.3, must be addressed.

The use of a physician extender, or "telepresenter" as he or she may also be described, can be a significant boost to efficiency in the delivery of telehealth services, while also increasing patient convenience. On the other hand, use of a telepresenter does create an additional step and, if not a required step, may create more burden than benefit. In the past, many states' telehealth laws required the use of telepresenter in the course of a telehealth consultation. Most states including Alaska, Hawaii, and, most recently, Texas have repealed such requirements in the last several years.

2.2.2.3 Direct-to-Consumer Communication

The direct-to-consumer (D2C) model is just that—a telehealth model based upon direct communication between a provider and a consumer. No other providers or telepresenters are present with the patient. This can be a key "value add" for providing "on demand" and convenient health care. The ability for consumers to "see a doctor now" is often touted as resulting in higher patient satisfaction with their health care services. In direct-to-consumer models, consumers, through technologies on mobile apps, websites, etc., can connect with a provider from just about anywhere. Parents who do not want to transport sick children, and people who simply feel too sick to leave the house, view the ability to access care from home as the most convenient feature of the D2C model. Employers are increasingly offering D2C telehealth models as a benefit under their health plans and may provide telehealth "kiosks" at their business locations. D2C telehealth connections are also appearing in malls, airports, and schools, not only for the benefit of employees at those locations but also for patrons, travelers, and students.

In a D2C model, consumers connect with providers who have agreed to be available to respond to consumer requests for services. D2C telehealth providers may be subject to response time requirements, as users in this model often require more immediate service. Consumers utilizing D2C telehealth often cannot timely readily access a health care provider in a facility, and use telehealth primarily for its on-demand function. Most often the provider and consumer have not had a prior interaction, (i.e., established a provider/patient relationship). In the absence of such a relationship, consumers are often directed to receive any necessary follow-up from their existing provider or to find a local provider who can provide the necessary care. Other D2C models enable consumers to directly connect with their existing provider or provider group. In these models, the consumer is an existing patient of the provider or group practice, such that there is less uncertainty as to the provision of follow-up care.

While D2C most commonly offers on-demand services, some D2C models offer the option of scheduling future appointments. The advance scheduling option is likely selected when choice of provider is more important than the immediacy of the consultation.

Given the absence of a telepresenter with the patient in most D2C models, consideration should be given to the type of information that should be disseminated to consumers prior to commencing a telehealth consultation.

2.2.3 Remote Patient Monitoring

Through remote patient monitoring (RPM), patient data is collected and transmitted through an electronic connection to providers in remote locations. The providers are tasked with monitoring and assessing the patient's current health status and, based on the data, making any recommendations for interventions, modifications in care protocols, etc. Data collected runs the gamut, but common examples include vital signs, breathing patterns, wound care progression, heart rate, and blood pressure. The monitoring health care providers can be in a variety of locations, including hospitals, nursing facilities, physician practices or off-site centralized monitoring facilities. RPM can be performed in patients' homes or in a health care facility setting. Many states include RPM in their definition of *telehealth* or *telemedicine*. With respect to Medicaid coverage, many state Medicaid programs provide reimbursement for remote patient monitoring, though some limit the reimbursement to monitoring for certain conditions, such as congestive heart failure, COPD, asthma or diabetes (as in Colorado), or for certain services such as skilled nursing home visits (as in Minnesota).[7]

Asserted benefits of RPM include early detection and intervention of medical issues before they become critical, reduction in hospital admissions or emergency room visits and improvement in the quality of life of patients who are allowed to remain in their own homes. RPM may provide the most benefit to chronically ill patients (e.g., congestive heart failure, pulmonary disease (COPD) patients) who require constant management, which, historically, could be provided only within a facility setting. Proponents also highlight RPM as an approach to keeping the elderly population in their homes. Given these benefits, states that do not currently reimburse for or recognize RPM may soon reevaluate that position. Kentucky, for example, recently passed legislation to establish a pilot project creating coverage and reimbursement criteria for "telemonitoring" services.[8] Medicare has yet to include RPM as a reimbursable modality. However, recent expansion of reimbursement for management of chronic care via non-face-to-face encounters indicates that CMS recognizes the benefits of remote management of the chronically ill. Further, there have been numerous government mandates for studying the impact and benefits of RPM, which indicate that the government has not written it off yet as a viable and legitimate telehealth service delivery model.

2.3 Telehealth Practice Requirements

When discussing the "practice" of telehealth, it's important to consider nuances among the various terms used. A licensed health care professional's *scope of practice* is commonly understood to describe "what" services the professional can render, while the professional's *standard of practice* is understood to be "how" the professional renders the service. Ethical principles are embodied in the professional's standard of practice. State laws and professional societies, such as the AMA and FSMB, generally consider a professionals scope of practice and standard of practice to be the same in the in-person setting as in the telehealth setting. For example, the AMA, in its 2016 Telemedicine Guidelines (AMA Guidelines), and the FSMB, in its Model Guidelines for State Medical Boards

[7] 10 CCR 2505-10:8.525 (2017); Minnesota Provider Manual—Home Care Services (2015).

[8] Ky. Rev. Stat. Ann. § 205.632 (2016).

(FSMB Model Guidelines), emphasize that physicians engaging in telemedicine must meet the requirements of the traditional standards of care. This specifically includes appropriately establishing a relationship with the patient and conducting evaluations with appropriate consideration of the patient's condition. Similarly, Colorado law provides that "any act or omission in the practice of telemedicine that fails to meet generally accepted standards of medical practice" constitutes unprofessional conduct.[9] Many view this position as legitimizing the practice of telehealth by equating it to traditional in-person services.

Nevertheless, there is still the "separate-but-equal" regulation of telemedicine. State have published guidance or promulgated laws specific to telehealth. These guidance documents often impose telehealth-specific practice requirements, including the establishment of the provider/patient relationship, informed consent, the location of the provider or patient, and/or the technology used.

2.3.1 Provider-Patient Relationship

The relationship between a provider and patient is the foundation of medical or clinical practice. Certain obligations and privileges trigger once that relationship commences, as does risk of professional liability. However, in the absence of a properly formed patient relationship, professionals are at risk for participation in the unauthorized practice of their profession. For these and other reasons, it is imperative that all telehealth providers clearly understand when the patient relationship commences.

Within the medical profession, the relationship exists when a physician services a patient's medical needs.[9] The FSMB recognizes that this may be difficult to ascertain when the patient and physician are in different locations but asserts that the relationship "tends to begin when an individual with a health-related matter seeks assistance from a physician who may provide assistance . . . [and] when the physician agrees to undertake diagnosis and treatment of the patient and the patient agrees to be treated . . . ."[10] According to the FSMB, this relationship can commence and continue even in the absence of an in-person encounter between the physician and patient; however, many states take a different view.

2.3.1.1 Pre-existing Relationship vs. Establishing Relationship via Telehealth

As discussed above, the establishment of the patient relationship is the core of medical and other clinical practices. In the context of telehealth, the question is whether or not this relationship can be *established* via a telehealth examination or visit or whether the relationship must be established via an in-person visit.

Following a recent change in Texas law, there are currently no states that explicitly prohibit the establishment of a provider-patient relationship via telehealth. However, several states have statutory requirements that may effectively make it difficult to establish a provider-patient relationship via telehealth,[11] and/or have indicated through informal guidance or communications that they interpret the statutory requirements as necessitating an in-person examination.[12]

Many states explicitly permit the establishment of a provider-patient relationship via telehealth, subject to the states' requirements with respect to permitted communication modalities (e.g., real-time audio/video vs. store and forward). For example, Maine's telemedicine practice guidelines clearly establish that a patient relationship can be established via telemedicine, but specifies that a

---

[9] Colo. Rev. Stat. § 12-36-117(1)(jj) (2013).

[9] Am. Med. Ass'n, 2016 Telemedicine Guidelines § 1.1.1 (2016) (hereinafter AMA *Guidelines*).

[10] FSMB Model Policy, *supra*, § 2.

[11] *See* Ga. Comp. R. & Regs. r. 360-3-.07.

[12] *See* N.J. Admin. Code § 13:35-7.1A(a).

static internet questionnaire provided to the patient cannot serve to establish the physician-patient relationship.[13] Maryland law does not require a face-to-face encounter to create a physician-patient relationship provided that evaluations are conducted via real-time audio *or* audio and video communication.[14]

In Oklahoma, telemedicine physicians are specifically exempted from the face-to-face evaluation requirement for creating a physician-patient relationship, provided certain requirements are met.[15] In addition, Alaska law permits physicians to diagnose, treat, or prescribe a drug (with the exception of controlled substances) without a physical examination, *if* the physician *or other health care provider* is available for follow-up care and the physician requests that the person consent to sending a copy of all records of the encounter to the person's primary care provider.[16] Under the Illinois Insurance Code, payors covering telehealth services are prohibited from requiring in-person contact between a provider and patient as well as requiring a provider to document why an in-person consultation was not possible. Illinois law also prohibits payors from imposing requirements to the contrary, such as requiring the use of telehealth if a patient chooses an in-person consultation.[17]

Some state requirements for face-to-face evaluations are specialty specific. For example, in Ohio, while there is no specific in-person evaluation requirement for physicians, social workers must conduct an initial in-person evaluation.[18] Similarly, in West Virginia, a physician-patient relationship can be established through store and forward technology for pathology and radiology, but there is not a similar allowance for other specialties.[19]

Typically, state laws require that the telehealth encounter meet current standards of care and that any technologies used are sufficient to allow for accurate treatment and diagnosis in accordance with that standard of care. Such "standards" commonly include: (a) a properly licensed physician; (b) the performance of a history and physical examination; (c) appropriate diagnostic testing; and (d) the creation of appropriate health care records.[20]

As with in-person visits, the requirement for a physician-patient relationship often contains exceptions for intermittent consultations or emergencies. For example, in Delaware, telemedicine visits may be provided without a physician-patient relationship in the case of an: (a) informal and infrequent consultation performed by a physician who is not compensated for such; (b) emergencies when the physician does not charge for services; and (c) episodic consultations by a physician in a different location upon request from a treating provider.[21]

2.3.1.2 Provider/Patient Validation

While states may allow for the establishment of a provider/patient relationship via telemedicine, some "telemedicine-specific" practice requirements require, among other things, validation of the provider and patient.

In the bricks-and-mortar setting, patients enter an office, interact with clinical and administrative staff, and perhaps interact with or observe other patients. Each of these factors, in one way or the

---

[13] 02-373-6 Me. Code R. § 3 (2016).

[14] Md. Code Regs. § 10.32.05.05.

[15] Okla. Admin. Code § 435:10-7-13 (2014).

[16] Alaska Stat. § 08.64.364 (2016); 2016 Alaska Sess. Laws ch. 25 (S.B. 74).

[17] 215 Ill. Comp. Stat. 5/356Z.22 (2015).

[18] Ohio Admin. Code 4757-5-13 (2016).

[19] W. Va. Code § 30-14-12d (2016).

[20] *See, e.g.*, S.C. Code Ann. § 40-47-37 (2016).

[21] Del. Code Ann. tit. 24, § 1769D (2015).

other, validates the existence of the provider and the provider's practice. Similarly, the patient's disclosure of his or her personal information and history gives the provider a detailed picture of the patient through body language and information gathered regarding the issues necessitating the request for health care. Likely in support of parity with the bricks-and-mortar setting, validation occurs in the telehealth setting through provider disclosure and patient-specific requirements. For example, providers must know the patient's location to confirm it is a jurisdiction in which they are licensed to practice. Obtaining the patient's location in advance can be helpful from a billing and reimbursement perspective, such as when a state's Medicaid program only reimburses for telehealth services provided to patients in certain rural or other specified areas. There may also be the perception that telehealth interactions lack some of the controls of an in-person consultation, which may lead patients to view telehealth as an opportunity to obtain medications fraudulently or services under a stolen identify.

For these reasons, many states require that providers properly and completely disclose their name, location and credentials (e.g., physician, physician assistant, nurse practitioner) to the patient.[22] Providers often also are required to validate the patient's identity through the display of identification or other personal information and the patient's location. Many states, such as Mississippi, expressly include such validation as a required step to the process of establishing the patient-relationship.[23] They also are required part of the telehealth informed consent process. The patient and provider validation process can also be incorporated into technology requirements. For example, Maine has express requirements for telehealth technology, one of which being that it has the capability to verify the identity of both the provider and the patient.[24]

2.3.1.3 Informed Consent

Health care professionals, particularly physicians, are familiar with the concept of informed consent and their obligation to provide patients with information related to the benefits, risks and costs of a particular treatment.[25] Physicians generally are permitted to exercise professional judgment in determining the content of such informed consent. In the telehealth world, however, informed consent requirements can more proscriptive. Both the FSMB and the AMA have mandated baseline elements for informed consent in the telehealth context, including:

Patients' Rights:

- To refuse to receive services via telehealth without it impacting their ability to receive any other future health care services.
- To validate and identify the provider's credentials (see prior discussion).

Providers' Obligations:

- To identify the patient and the patient's location (see prior discussion).
- To disclose any financial interests the provider may have in the telemedicine application, technology, or hardware.
- To inform the patient how to obtain follow-up care.
- To instruct the patient to notify his/her primary care physician about the telemedicine consult. This supports the continuity of care and further ensures the patient receives follow-up care.

---

[22] S.C. Code Ann. § 40-47-37 (2016).

[23] 30-17 Miss. Admin. Code § 2635 (5.4) (2013).

[24] 02-373-6 Me. Code R. § 3 (2016).

[25] AMA Guidelines, *supra*, § 1.1.3.

- To describe how the patient can obtain records of the telehealth service and assert that the information can be sent to the patient's other providers upon request.
- To disclose the types of communications and transmissions that are and are not permitted using telehealth technologies (e.g., controlled drug substance prescriptions, prescription refills, appointment scheduling, urgent or emergent care, patient education, etc.).
- To assert that it is the physician and not the patient who determines whether the condition being diagnosed and/or treated is appropriate for a telehealth service and that the physician can direct the patient to seek care elsewhere if telehealth is deemed not appropriate.
- To provide details on security measures in place related to the use of telehealth technologies. Examples include encryption of data, password-protected screen savers and data files, or the utilization of other reliable authentication techniques.
- To disclose potential privacy risks that exist, despite the institution of security measures.
- To assert that the provider cannot guarantee consistent, uninterrupted performance of the technologies, with an agreement that the provider will be held harmless for information lost due to technical failures, such as internet connectivity.
- To obtain express patient consent to forward patient-identifiable information to a third party.
- To explain fees for services and how payment is made.[26]

Almost half of the states have some form of informed consent law, and the majority of those incorporate at least some, if not all of the elements of FSMB's and AMA's informed consent.

Some states, such as Arizona and California, allow certain information to be disclosed in either verbal or written format. Some states, such as Colorado, require that the information be disclosed in writing, and some, such as Nebraska, require written consent signed by the patient.[27] Regardless of whether the consent is provided in a verbal or written form, most states require documentation that informed consent has been provided. Even if not expressly required, documenting the receipt of informed consent is commonly agreed upon as a best practice in the telehealth arena.

State laws also may differ regarding the party responsible for obtaining informed consent. Most states' informed consent obligations fall on the telemedicine providers. However, others impose it on the referring provider, i.e., the provider referring for the telemedicine consult, as is the case under Georgia Medicaid rules, and/or on the originating site, as does Maryland.[28] In a further variation, sometimes the consent requirement applies only to telehealth services provided using asynchronous store and forward technology, such as in Missouri and Vermont.[29] With respect to teledermatology and teleophthalmology, Vermont law requires that patients be informed of the right to receive a consultation with the distant site health care provider and that receiving teledermatology or teleophthalmology by store and forward means shall not preclude a patient from receiving real-time telemedicine or face-to-face services with the distant site health care provider at a future date.

---

[26] FSMB Model Guidelines, *supra*; AMA Guidelines, *supra*.

[27] Ariz. Rev. Stat. Ann § 36-3602 (2016); Cal. Bus. & Prof. Code § 2290.5 (2016); Colo. Rev. Stat. § 25.5-5-320 (2008); Neb. Rev. Stat. § 71-8505(2) (1999).

[28] Ga. Dep't of Cmty. Health, Div. of Medicaid, Georgia Telemedicine Guide 5 (2016); Md. Dep't of Health & Mental Hygiene, Md. Medicaid Telehealth Program Telehealth Provider Manual 1, 5, 6 (2016).

[29] Mo. Rev. Stat. § 208.671 (2016); Vt. Stat. Ann. tit. 18, § 9361 (2012).

On the other end of the spectrum, Indiana law prohibits requirements that health care providers obtain a separate written consent for the provision of health care services via telemedicine services.[30]

The final point to make about informed consent is that some view it as a misnomer. Many in the industry view the telehealth-specific informed consent to be distinct from the type of informed consent required prior to a health care procedure. Often, telemedicine informed consents are described as a disclosure or recognition and acknowledgement.

2.3.2 Additional In-Person Evaluation Requirements

Related to the issue of establishing a provider-patient relationship via telehealth is the issue of whether, once a patient relationship has been established, there is any need or requirement for future in-person services. As with the establishment of a provider-patient relationship, statutory requirements for in-person evaluations of established patients are increasingly rare, although typically this flexibility is subject to a telehealth encounter being able to satisfy the applicable standard of care for the diagnosis or treatment in question. For example, California prohibits health plans from requiring in-person examinations, while acknowledging the provider may exercise professional judgment and determine an in-person visit is appropriate.[31]

Some states, while not explicitly requiring in-person evaluations by the telehealth provider, do create obligations on a telehealth provider to ensure the patient has access to in-person care by an appropriate provider. For example, Georgia law requires a telehealth provider to make "diligent efforts" to have the patient seen in person by an appropriate provider.[32]

2.3.3 Patient/Provider Type and Location Requirements

Another telehealth practice requirement pertains to the location of the provider, patient or both. This requirement applies to Medicare coverage and often applies to Medicaid coverage, as further discussed in Chapter 3. A trend in state law has been to remove limitations on patient/originating and provider/distant locations. For example, California and Louisiana do not impose any location requirement on the patient or provider, allowing either to be in any location.[33] In addition, Oregon prohibits insurance plans from distinguishing between originating sites that are rural or urban in providing coverage.[34] The most common limitation on location is to disqualify a patient's home from being an originating site. Under these circumstances, RPM, as discussed previously is not a permissible telehealth model.

Hawaii's Medicaid statute limits originating sites to facilities (hospital, critical access hospital, FQHC, and federal telehealth demonstration cites) and to locations that are demonstration project sites, HPSAs, or outside of a metropolitan statistical area (MSA).[35] Similarly, many states, such as Michigan, Washington, and Wyoming, limit originating and, though less often, distant sites to specific provider types under applicable Medicaid statutes.[36]

---

[30] Ind. Code § 16-36-1-15 (2015).

[31] Cal. Health & Safety Code § 1374.13 (2013).

[32] Ga. Comp. R. & Regs. 360-3-.07(a)(8) (2014).

[33] Cal. Health and Safety Code § 1374.13 (2013); La. Stat. Ann. § 37:1271(4)(a) (2016).

[34] Or. Rev. Stat § 743A.058 (2015).

[35] Haw. Code R. § 17-1737-51.1 (2005).

[36] Mich. Dep't of Health & Human Servs., Medicaid Provider Manual § 17.3 (2017); Rev. Code of Wash. §§ 41.05.700, 48.43.735 & 74.09.325 (2017); Wyo. Dep't of Health, Div. of Healthcare Fin., CMS 1500 ICD-10 104 (2016).

2.3.4 Technology Requirements

Technology is at the center of telehealth, as without technology there would be no telehealth. While a facilitator, however, telehealth technology is also a risk area. The seamless use of any telehealth model depends on the seamless operation of the telehealth technology. Accordingly, it is not surprising that some states regulate and restrict the types of telehealth technologies that may be used. Such regulation often goes beyond synchronistic v. asynchronistic and gets into the details of the technology's capabilities.

For example, Maryland law requires that telehealth technologies have: (1) a camera with specific resolution, focus, and zoom capabilities; (2) a display monitor sufficient in size; (3) bandwidth speed and image resolution sufficient to provide quality video; (4) audio equipment that ensures clear communication; and (5) audio transmission with less than 300 millisecond delay.[37] In addition to requiring real time interactive video, Oklahoma requires the technology to be compliant with HIPAA's security standards.[38]

Similarly, Maine's rules for telehealth practice require that the technology: (1) comply with all relevant safety laws, rules, regulations, and codes for technology and technical safety for devices that interact with patients or are integral to diagnostic capabilities; (2) be of sufficient quality, size, resolution and clarity such that the licensee can safely and effectively provide the telemedicine services; (3) be compliant with HIPAA; (4) be capable of verifying the identity and location of the patient; and (5) be capable of specifying and disclosing the identity and credentials of the health care provider(s). The last two requirements highlight Maine's requirement for provider/patient validation as discussed above.[39]

2.4 Vulnerable Patient Populations

Special consideration should be given to populations viewed as vulnerable with respect to their ability to understand the specifics of their health care. Telemedicine models should incorporate specific processes and safeguards for minors and incapacitated adults who seek services via telemedicine.

As in the in-person setting, if a telehealth provider reasonably suspects that a patient lacks the ability to make decisions for him- or herself, whether due to age or mental capacity, the provider should take steps to validate or disprove that suspicion. Telehealth providers can easily resolve the question in the case of minors by requesting a copy of the patient's birth certificate. It is not as simple in the context of incapacitated adults, as the provider must rely on his or her professional judgment. If a provider validates a patient's lack of legal capacity or, based on his or her professional judgment, believes the patient to lack capacity, the next step is for the provider to identify an authorized decision maker and obtain that person's consent. For example, Nebraska's telemedicine law expressly requires that patients who are minors or mentally incompetent have a parent or guardian sign the required written consent.[40]

In the in-person setting, providers often have more regulator contact with a patient, allowing them to accumulate information related to the patient's caregiver or guardian status—through factual information such as insurance coverage, or patterns of activity such as who regularly accompanies the patient to appointments. In the context of telehealth, interactions may be more sporadic, and knowledge regarding a caregiver or guardian is not as easily ascertained. Therefore, telehealth

---

[37] Md. Dep't of Health & Mental Hygiene, Md. Medicaid Telehealth Program Telehealth Provider Manual 4 (2016).

[38] Okla. Admin. Code § 435:10-7-13 (2014).

[39] 02-373-6 Me. Code R. § 15 (2016).

[40] Neb. Rev. Stat. § 71-8505(3) (1999).

providers should have a process in place for validating a decision maker's authority. For example, providers may want to require primary source documentation, such as a birth certificate or driver's license as part of their intake process. In the case of an incapacitated adult, substantiation of legal authority can be even harder to assess; providers therefore may want to require copies of legal documentation, such as a power of attorney.

Minors who have been emancipated under state law have the ability to make all health care decisions on their own behalf. In the face of a minor patient's assertion of emancipation, providers should request supporting legal documentation. Further, in some states, minors can independently consent to certain health care services, such as substance abuse treatment and birth control. Providers should be familiar with their state's specific laws in this area, as requiring the involvement of a parent or guardian in these situations would not be appropriate.

2.5 Non-Physician Providers and Telehealth

Much of state law, regulation, and guidance regarding the use of telehealth has been specific to the practice of medicine by physicians, raising the inevitable question of whether, and under what circumstances, allied health professionals may use telehealth in the delivery of services within their scope of practice.

The use of telehealth by allied health professionals raises a number of unique considerations given the supervision and collaboration requirements frequently imposed on non-physician providers. As a result, the ability of a particular allied health professional to provide telehealth services may depend in part on the particular licensure category applicable to such non-physician provider.

2.5.1 Provider Categories

Allied health professionals fall into several distinct categories both with respect to licensure and scope of practice as well as the degree of autonomy and independence they have in the provision of services. Allied health professional typically fall within one of the following categories:

- Advanced practice nurse (APN), including nurse practitioners, nurse anesthetists, nurse midwives, and clinical nurse specialists
- Physician assistant (PA)
- Registered nurses (RN)
- Medical assistants (MA)

Allied health professionals generally can be further categorized into "independent practitioners" and "dependent practitioners." Independent practitioners typically are permitted to practice independently of a physician, subject to the services falling within the practitioner's scope of practice. Dependent practitioners must work under the direct supervision of a physician. APNs are typically classified as independent practitioners, however the degree of independence and requirements for physician involvement vary among states, including with respect to prescribing authority. On the other end of the spectrum, RNs and MAs are dependent practitioners who typically must perform services under the direct supervision of a physician (or in some cases, an APN), and may not prescribe medications. PAs typically cannot practice independently, however, they often have some level of prescribing authority.

2.5.2 Telehealth Practice Standards

The provision of professional services by allied health professionals is regulated at the state level. Statutes governing the use of telehealth generally, regulations, and guidance promulgated by state licensing boards, and statutes and regulations governing the prescription of drugs all can include requirements for the use of telehealth by allied health professionals. Likewise state Medicaid statutes can establish requirements applicable to reimbursement for telehealth services. However, while almost all states have promulgated some form of telehealth statutes, regulations or other guidance with respect to the practice of medicine, these do not always specifically extend to or otherwise consider the use of telehealth by non-physician providers. This makes it difficult to know the extent to which a particular category of allied health professional may use telehealth and/or the standards applicable to such services. Moreover, in states where the rules or regulations are left to the discretion of applicable licensing boards, the guidance available for allied health professionals is often less comprehensive than that available for physicians.

In states that have adopted statutes that address the issue of telehealth generally, the statutes themselves often cover a number of different license categories. California made the provisions of the California Telehealth Advancement Act of 2011 applicable to all "health care providers" licensed under Division 2 of the California Business and Professions Code, which include, among others, nurses and physician assistants.[41] Similarly, Connecticut[42] and Indiana[43] have rules that apply to a number of categories of health care professionals, including advanced practice registered nurses and physician assistants. Taking a slightly different approach, Florida telehealth regulations specifically apply to physicians and physician assistants, but do not address other categories of allied health professionals.[44]

States sometimes address telehealth generally by statute, but then either direct or permit certain licensing boards to develop appropriate rules governing its use. Louisiana has taken such an approach, providing that each state agency or professional or occupational licensing board that regulates the practice of a health care provider may promulgate rules consistent with its telehealth statute.[45] Missouri, through an amendment to its Nursing Practice Act in 2013, tasked the State Board of Registration for the Healing Arts and the State Board of Nursing jointly to promulgate rules governing the practice of telehealth by nurses more broadly.[46]

In other states, the use of telehealth by a particular category of provider is addressed individually under the licensing statutes, regulations or rules applicable to such category of provider. In some cases, this has led to statutory inconsistencies with respect to how telehealth may be used by a physician vs. a non-physician provider, which can be challenging for telehealth providers seeking to make the services of both physicians and non-physician providers available through the same practice or telehealth platform. For example, in its regulations governing the use of telehealth by physicians, Delaware has made clear that, absent a prior in-person examination or the presence of a licensed practitioner at the originating site, and excluding certain specialties, a telehealth encounter must use "real time" audio and video technology.[47] In contrast, while Delaware's regulations

---

[41] *See* Cal. Health & Safety Code § 2290.5.

[42] *See* Conn. Gen. Stat. § 19a-906(d).

[43] *See* Ind. Code §§ 25-1-9.5.

[44] *See* Fla. Admin. Code § 64B8-9.0141(8).

[45] *See* La. R.S. §§ 40:1300.401 *et seq.*

[46] *See* Mo. Rev. Stat. § 335.175.

[47] *See* 24 Del. Code § 1769(D)(h).

governing the use of telehealth by an advanced practice registered nurse contains a number of requirements that parallel its physician telehealth statute, it does not specifically address the use of real-time audio/video technology.[48]

Some jurisdictions have not adopted any statutes or rules specific to the use of telehealth by allied health professionals, but include certain allied health professionals within the categories of providers covered by reimbursement parity laws and/or Medicaid reimbursement statutes. For example, the District of Columbia has not yet adopted any statutes or regulations governing the use of telehealth generally and relies upon the District of Columbia Board of Medicine's Telemedicine Policy governing the provision of telehealth services by physicians.[49] But the District has adopted a telehealth reimbursement parity law that applies beyond physicians to include "health care practitioners."[50]

Some states provide only informal guidance for the use of telehealth by allied health professionals. For example, in North Carolina, where telehealth is regulated primarily through state medical board guidance and pharmacy statutes, the state's Board of Nursing has addressed the use of telehealth by nurses informally through FAQs and position statements that do not have the force and effect of law.[51] Similarly, in Iowa, the Board of Nursing has provided limited guidance through FAQs made available as part of the Board's position statements.[52]

Ultimately, allied health professionals must look to multiple statutory and regulatory sources to determine whether they are permitted to use telehealth in the delivery of services and, if so, what standards may apply to their provision of services via telehealth. In the absence of specific statutory or regulatory guidance addressing the use of telehealth by allied health professionals in a given state, allied health professionals will need to seek informal guidance from their professional licensing boards to determine the appropriate use of telehealth within their licensure and scope of practice.

2.5.3 Supervision Requirements

As noted above, allied health professionals have varying degrees of independence based upon their category of licensure as well as the state in which they practice. Dependent practitioners generally are required to provide services under the supervision of a physician licensed within the state in which the patient is located. Even independently practicing APNs are sometimes *required* to be supervised to some degree by a physician licensed in the state and/or require licensed physician involvement through a collaboration agreement setting forth the scope of the APN's authority and/or the parameters of supervision. According to the American Association of Nurse Practitioners, 23 states allow APNs to evaluate, diagnose, and provide treatment, including the prescription of medication, under the exclusive authority of the state board of nursing, with the remaining states limiting to some degree the ability of APNs to practice independently.[53] The specific requirements for supervision and/or collaboration applicable to a given allied health professional are established on a state-by-state basis, and can vary even within states depending upon the particular action being taken (e.g., prescribing, or prescribing a particular class of drugs).

---

48 *See id.* § 1933.

49 *See* D.C. Bd. of Med., Policy No. 15-01, Telemedicine Policy (Nov. 13, 2014).

50 *See* D.C. Code §§ 31-3131(7); 31-31861 et. seq.

51 *See* N.C. Bd. of Nursing Position Statement for RN and LPN Practice, http://www.ncbon.com/myfiles/downloads/position-statements-decision-trees/telehealth-telenursing.pdf; N.C. Bd. of Nursing FAQ—Nurse Practitioner, http://www.ncbon.com/dcp/i/nursing-practice-nurse-practitioner-faq--nurse-practitioner-np-1#faq28.

52 *See* Position Statements and Papers Adopted by the Iowa Bd. of Nursing, Provision of Nursing Services by Telehealth/Electronic means, https://nursing.iowa.gov/practice/position-statements-and-papers-adopted-iowa-board-nursing/provision-nursing-services.

53 *See* https://www.aanp.org/legislation-regulation/state-legislation/state-practice-environment.

Supervision requirements can further complicate or, in some cases, effectively prohibit the use of telehealth in certain care delivery models when such requirements cannot be satisfied through remote supervision. Supervision requirements were developed and adopted in the context of in-person care in which the physical presence of a physician at or near the point of care was assumed. Most do not contemplate today's technology-driven world, in which providers have the ability to deliver both medical care and supervision remotely.

While many states do not specifically address whether supervision may be provided remotely, some states retain in-person or physical proximity requirements relating to supervision than can impact the use of telehealth. For example, Missouri requires that in any collaborative practice arrangement in which the collaborating physician is not continuously physically present, the APN and the collaborating physician must practice together at the same location with the collaborating physician continuously present for a period of at least one month before the APN may practice without the presence of the collaborating physician.[54] In the case of the diagnosis or treatment of acutely or chronically ill or injured patients, Missouri further requires that, subject to certain limited exceptions, a collaborating physician who supervises an APN from a different location be located within 30 miles of the APN.[55] Perhaps recognizing the challenges such geographic proximity requirements create for the use of telehealth, Missouri created certain exceptions to its proximity requirements for circumstances in which the physician and APN utilize telehealth, but only if the telehealth services are provided in a "rural area of need."[56] In a somewhat less restrictive model, Tennessee requires a physician supervising an APN visit any remote site at least once every 30 days and be available (or make arrangements for a substitute physician to be available) for consultation at all times.[57] Such restrictions can prove limiting or prohibitive for providers offering services exclusively or primarily via telehealth. For example, direct-to-consumer telehealth platforms may utilize providers located in multiple jurisdictions with no physical sites that enable them to satisfy such requirements.

Even in states that do not have specific geographic or in-person supervision requirements, the issue of whether remote supervision is permissible is often not entirely clear. For example, in Arizona, unprofessional conduct of a physician includes "lack of or inappropriate direction, collaboration or direct supervision of a medical assistant or a licensed, certified or registered health care provider employed by, supervised by or assigned to the physician;"[58] however, the statute does not define what constitutes "direct" supervision.

In addition to statutes, regulations and rules governing supervision of allied health professionals more generally, providers who seek reimbursement from commercial or state Medicaid payors must also be aware of standards relating to supervision that could impact reimbursement. For example, in Massachusetts an APN must have a written supervision arrangement with a MassHealth-participating physician in the APN's "service area"[59] to obtain Medicaid reimbursement.

Finally, even in states where APNs may practice independently, providers must be mindful of those patient services that may nonetheless require supervision (and the parameters for such supervision).

---

[54] *See* Mo. 20 CSR 2200-4.200(C).

[55] *Id.* at 2200-4.200(2)(B).

[56] *See* Mo. Nursing Practice Act § 335.175.

[57] *See* Tenn. Comp. R & Regs. r. 0880-6-.02(2)-(3).

[58] Ariz. Rev. Stat. § 32-1401(27)(ii).

[59] MassHealth Provider Manual 433.433.

Given the explosion of legislative activity among the states with respect to telehealth more generally, it is likely only a matter of time before state nursing boards and legislators address the varied questions that arise with respect to the use of remote supervision. Providers will need to keep abreast of specific guidance and developments applicable to the states in which they practice.

2.6 Remote Prescribing

In addition to reviewing state statutes and regulations governing the use of telehealth, providers also must consider restrictions or requirements that apply to the issuance of a prescription based upon a remote telehealth encounter. As with telehealth standards more generally, prescribing requirements are largely promulgated at the state level. However, the federal government also has imposed certain limitations on prescriptions issued to individuals remotely through the Ryan Haight Online Pharmacy Consumer Protection Act of 2008 (Ryan Haight Act) and its implementing regulations.

2.6.1 Ryan Haight Act

Congress enacted the Ryan Haight Act in 2008 following the death of Ryan Haight, a teenager who had obtained Vicodin through an online pharmacy. The Ryan Haight Act amended the Controlled Substances Act to add restrictions on the distribution of controlled substances via the internet. Under the Ryan Haight Act, it is unlawful for any person to "knowingly or intentionally" deliver, distribute or dispense a controlled substance through the internet without a "valid prescription," or "aid or abet" in such activity, unless an applicable exception is satisfied.[60]

A "valid prescription" requires that the prescribing provider have conducted at least one in-person medical evaluation of the patient that was conducted in the physical presence of the prescribing provider, or that the prescribing provider be a "covering practitioner," who conducts a medical evaluation (other than in-person) at the request of a provider (1) who is temporarily unavailable to conduct such evaluation and (2) previously conducted at least one in-person medical evaluation of the patient.[61]

The Ryan Haight Act exempts prescriptions that are issued and dispensed pursuant to "the practice of telemedicine," however, the parameters for what qualifies as the "practice of telemedicine" under the Ryan Haight Act have effectively prevented the prescription of controlled substances through a telehealth encounter unless the provider previously conducted an in-person evaluation of the patient.[62]

---

[60] 21 U.S.C. § 841(h).

[61] *See id.* § 829(e).

[62] The "practice of telemedicine" exempted under the Ryan Haight Act is limited to the following:

"[T]he practice of medicine in accordance with applicable Federal and State laws by a practitioner (other than a pharmacist) who is at a location remote from the patient and is communicating with the patient, or health care professional who is treating the patient, using a telecommunications system referred to in section 1395m(m) of title 42, which practice—

(A) is being conducted—

(i) while the patient is being treated by, and physically located in, a hospital or clinic registered under section 823(f) of this title; and

(ii) by a practitioner—

(I) acting in the usual course of professional practice;

(II) acting in accordance with applicable State law; and

(III) registered under section 823(f) of this title in the State in which the patient is located, unless the practitioner—

(aa) is exempted from such registration in all States under section 822(d) of this title; or

(Text continued on page 61)

(bb) is—

(AA) an employee or contractor of the Department of Veterans Affairs who is acting in the scope of such employment or contract; and

(BB) registered under section 823(f) of this title in any State or is utilizing the registration of a hospital or clinic operated by the Department of Veterans Affairs registered under section 823(f) of this title;

(B) is being conducted while the patient is being treated by, and in the physical presence of, a practitioner—

(i) acting in the usual course of professional practice;

(ii) acting in accordance with applicable State law; and

(iii) registered under section 823(f) of this title in the State in which the patient is located, unless the practitioner—

(I) is exempted from such registration in all States under section 822(d) of this title; or

(II) is—

(aa) an employee or contractor of the Department of Veterans Affairs who is acting in the scope of such employment or contract; and

(bb) registered under section 823(f) of this title in any State or is using the registration of a hospital or clinic operated by the Department of Veterans Affairs registered under section 823(f) of this title;

(C) is being conducted by a practitioner—

(i) who is an employee or contractor of the Indian Health Service, or is working for an Indian tribe or tribal organization under its contract or compact with the Indian Health Service under the Indian Self-Determination and Education Assistance Act [25 U.S.C. 450 *et seq.*];

(ii) acting within the scope of the employment, contract, or compact described in clause (i); and

(iii) who is designated as an Internet Eligible Controlled Substances Provider by the Secretary under section 831(g)(2) of this title;

(D) (i) is being conducted during a public health emergency declared by the Secretary under section 247d of title 42; and

(ii) involves patients located in such areas, and such controlled substances, as the Secretary, with the concurrence of the Attorney General, designates, provided that such designation shall not be subject to the procedures prescribed by subchapter II of chapter 5 of title 5;

(E) is being conducted by a practitioner who has obtained from the Attorney General a special registration under section 831(h) of this title;

(F) is being conducted—

(i) in a medical emergency situation—

(I) that prevents the patient from being in the physical presence of a practitioner registered under section 823(f) of this title who is an employee or contractor of the Veterans Health Administration acting in the usual course of business and employment and within the scope of the official duties or contract of that employee or contractor;

(II) that prevents the patient from being physically present at a hospital or clinic operated by the Department of Veterans Affairs registered under section 823(f) of this title;

(III) during which the primary care practitioner of the patient or a practitioner otherwise practicing telemedicine within the meaning of this paragraph is unable to provide care or consultation; and

(IV) that requires immediate intervention by a health care practitioner using controlled substances to prevent what the practitioner reasonably believes in good faith will be imminent and serious clinical consequences, such as further injury or death; and

(ii) by a practitioner that—

(I) is an employee or contractor of the Veterans Health Administration acting within the scope of that employment or contract;

(II) is registered under section 823(f) of this title in any State or is utilizing the registration of a hospital or clinic operated by the Department of Veterans Affairs registered under section 823(f) of this title; and

(III) issues a controlled substance prescription in this emergency context that is limited to a maximum of a 5-day

2.6.2 State-Based Requirements

At the state level, prescribing limitations may be imposed on prescribers through professional licensing statutes and regulations, as well as through requirements imposed on pharmacists in connection with dispensing medications. As a result, providers who desire to prescribe based upon remote telehealth encounters must be cognizant not only of the applicable telehealth or professional conduct requirements, but also any requirements imposed upon dispensing pharmacists that, as a practical matter, may prevent the issuance of a drug to a patient based upon a remote encounter.

Many states' statutes and regulations governing remote prescribing were implemented well before the technological capabilities and utilization of telehealth had advanced to enable the remote delivery of high quality care, and did not contemplate the nature of or degree to which, telehealth capabilities would change the way that providers and patients are able to interact. As with the Ryan Haight Act, the early focus of many states with respect to prescribing and telehealth was aimed at preventing the distribution of drugs through dubious online pharmacies As a result, many states' statutes and regulations specifically prohibit prescribing or dispensing based solely on an internet questionnaire or consultation or a telephonic consultation.[63] Alabama, Arkansas, Connecticut, District of Columbia, Idaho, Iowa, Kansas, Louisiana, Missouri, New Hampshire, New Jersey, New Mexico, Oregon, Vermont, West Virginia, and Wyoming all have language relating to internet-based questionnaires or telephonic consultation in their pharmacy statutes, regulations or guidance. While it is easy to imagine those extreme cases such language was originally intended to prevent (e.g., an internet pharmacy dispensing a dangerous drug based on a one page questionnaire), the language can be challenging in light of the technological capabilities of today's telehealth models, particularly because states generally do not provide specific standards or guidance with respect to what constitutes an internet questionnaire or evaluation. For example, if a direct-to-consumer online telemedicine platform solicits comprehensive information and history from a patient, including images, through a single online questionnaire that enables the prescriber to meet the standard of care, would such an interaction be deemed an internet questionnaire prohibited under an applicable statute?

As a practical matter, the answer to whether a prescription issued through a telehealth encounter is valid is often left to the discretion of the pharmacist dispensing the drug at issue. Pharmacy statutes and regulations governing the conduct of pharmacists often rely upon the judgment of the pharmacist, and pharmacy boards have disciplined pharmacists for failing to exercise appropriate judgment in dispensing drugs, even where the pharmacist's obligations are not entirely clear under the applicable statutory or regulatory guidance. For example, even though Minnesota's pharmacy statutes and regulations do not expressly prohibit prescriptions based upon an online encounter, the Minnesota pharmacy board has taken disciplinary action against pharmacists for dispensing drugs pursuant to prescriptions issued based on online questionnaires.[64]

Adding to the challenges is the fact that pharmacy statutes and regulations do not always line up with state legislative advancements regarding telehealth more generally. Some states, such as

---

supply which may not be extended or refilled; or

(G) is being conducted under any other circumstances that the Attorney General and the Secretary have jointly, by regulation, determined to be consistent with effective controls against diversion and otherwise consistent with the public health and safety."

See id. § 802(54).

[63] *See, e.g.*, Alabama, Arkansas, Connecticut, District of Columbia, Idaho, Iowa, Kansas, Louisiana, Missouri, New Hampshire, New Jersey, New Mexico, Oregon, Vermont, West Virginia, Wyoming.

[64] *See* Minn. Bd. of Pharmacy, Disciplinary Actions: [January 2001-April 2015].

Delaware[65] and Colorado,[66] have aligned their pharmacy statutes with the state's telehealth statutes and regulations. Others, such as Alaska, Hawaii Montana, Rhode Island and others, do not have any specific requirements in their pharmacy statutes relating to whether a prescription issued through a telehealth encounter is valid. However, there remain a number of states in which the pharmacy statutes and regulations or enforcement with respect to remote prescribing are not wholly consistent and/or create higher standards for issuing prescriptions based on telehealth encounters than are found in such state's requirements relating to face-to-face encounters. For example, in Louisiana, legislation adopted in 2016 establishes that a prior in-person encounter is not required to provide telemedicine provided the physician satisfies certain enumerated conditions relating to licensure, medical records and follow-up care.[67] However, Louisiana's pharmacy statutes and regulations prohibit a pharmacist from dispensing a prescription in the absence of a valid physician-patient relationship, which requires at least one in-person evaluation.[68]

Likewise, in the District of Columbia, guidance from the Board of Medicine indicates a prior in-person encounter is not required to provide telemedicine services provided that real-time auditory communications or real-time visual and auditory communications are used in the telemedicine encounter.[69] However, District of Columbia pharmacy regulations prohibit pharmacists from dispensing a prescription the pharmacist knows was issued without a valid patient-practitioner relationship, which under the pharmacy regulations require that the practitioner has met face-to-face with the patient.[70]

To the extent that a state has specific requirements relating to prescriptions based on remote encounters, these generally focus on the type of remote encounter between a prescriber and patient that is sufficient for prescribing; or, alternatively, what constitutes a "valid" prescription for purposes of dispensing. In some cases, the validity of the prescription is merely tied to it being issued by an appropriately licensed professional. For example, Georgia prohibits a pharmacist from dispensing a prescription the pharmacist "knows or should know is not a valid prescription," and defines validity based on whether the prescription was issued by a physician or other licensed professional.[71] Taking an even more hands off approach, Maryland simply provides that a prescription shall be "valid in the professional judgment of the pharmacist."[72] But many states have created more specific standards regarding the type of relationship or encounter sufficient for purposes of prescribing or dispensing drugs. These can create challenges for telehealth providers looking to prescribe based on remote encounters. The standards often focus on whether a provider-patient relationship exists, and how such a relationship may be established

Some states, such as the District of Columbia,[73] specify in their pharmacy statutes and regulations that, for purposes of prescribing, a valid provider-patient relationship requires an in-person encounter between the prescriber and the patient. In addition to requiring at least one in-person

---

[65] *See* Del. Code § 2502.

[66] *See* Colo. Code Regs. § 719-1:3.00.21.

[67] *See* La. Rev. Stat. Ann. § 37:1271(B)(2).

[68] *See* La. Rev. Stat. § 40:1060.16; La. Admin. Code tit. 46 § 2515.

[69] *See* D.C. Bd. of Med., Policy No. 15-01, Telemedicine Policy (Nov.13, 2014). *See also* Notice of Proposed Rulemaking—Establishing Rules on Telemedicine, http://www.dcregs.dc.gov/Gateway/NoticeHome.aspx?noticeid=5881612.

[70] *See* D.C. Mun. Regs. Tit. 22, §§ 1300.7, 1399.

[71] *See* Ga. Code § 26-4-80(b).

[72] *See* Md. Code Regs. 10.34.20.02.

[73] *Supra*, note 69.

medical evaluation,[74] Louisiana also provides a list of factors in its pharmacy regulations tending to show the absence of a valid physician-patient relationship, including the number of prescriptions authorized by a practitioner on a daily basis; the manner in which the prescriptions are authorized (e.g., electronically); the geographic distance between the practitioner and the patient; whether the prescription was issued solely as a result of answers to an electronic questionnaire; or whether the pharmacy directly or indirectly participates in an internet site that markets prescription drugs to the public.[75] In other cases, pharmacy statutes or regulations may require a pre-existing practitioner-patient relationship without specifying how such a relationship may be established. For example, Kentucky's pharmacy statute requires that a prescription, among other things, result from a valid practitioner-patient relationship.[76] The statute does not address how such practitioner-patient relationship lawfully may be established.

A number of states require that a prescription be based upon some form of physician examination or evaluation. These exam or evaluation requirements often result from the concept of a valid provider-patient relationship and may involve an in-person requirement, as in Louisiana and the District of Columbia. Likewise, the Arkansas Internet Prescription Consumer Protection Act specifies that, subject to certain limited exceptions, a "proper practitioner-patient relationship" requires that the provider have completed an in-person exam that is "adequate to establish a diagnosis and to identify underlying conditions or contraindications."[77] However, as with the question of how a provider-patient relationship may be established, many states' pharmacy statutes do not specify the form that the exam or evaluation must take, leaving open the question as to whether an exam or evaluation conducted through a remote telehealth encounter satisfies such standard. In such cases, the state's position with respect to telehealth more generally can be instructive in determining whether a remote exam or evaluation may suffice.

Even in states where prescribing based on a remote encounter generally is permitted, the type of drug being prescribed will in many cases determine whether a prescription may be issued or a drug dispensed based upon a remote encounter. Controlled substances are generally subject to a higher standard both under the Ryan Haight Act as well as state statutes and regulations. States frequently impose their own requirements on controlled substances and certain categories of drugs, including muscle relaxants and so-called "lifestyle" drugs (e.g., weight loss or erectile dysfunction drugs). These are typically more stringent than the state's requirements with respect to telehealth and/or prescribing more generally, and will often include an in-person examination or evaluation.[78]

2.7 Continuity of Care

The issue of how to ensure continuity of care for telehealth patients, including with respect to appropriate emergency services and follow-up care, has received attention from industry stakeholders but typically is not addressed in any detail in applicable state statutes and regulations. A number of states have included in their telehealth statutes and regulations general requirements relating to continuity of care. Likewise, organizations such as the Federation of State Medical Boards[79] and the American Medical Association[80] have addressed the need to include emergency and follow-up care

[74] *Supra*, note 68.

[75] *Id.*

[76] *See* Ky. Rev. Stat. § 315.010(22).

[77] *See* Ark. Code § 17-92-1003(15).

[78] *See* Minn. Stat. § 151.37(d), (e)., N.D. Cent. Code § 19.02.1-15.1(2).

[79] *See* Fed. State Med. Bds., "Model Policy for the Appropriate Use of Telemedicine Technologies in the Practice of Medicine (2014)," https://www.fsmb.org/Media/Default/PDF/FSMB/Advocacy/FSMB_Telemedicine_Policy.pdf.

[80] *See* American Medical Association, CMS Report 7-A-14.

in providers' policies and procedures. However, states and industry organizations have largely left the content and specifics of continuity of care policies and procedures to the discretion of providers. A number of states do not specifically address these issues at all. While the regulatory requirements related to continuity of care tend to be fairly general, the failure by a provider to develop and implement appropriate policies and procedures can create risk for the provider from both a liability and a regulatory perspective.

2.7.1 Emergency Care

In an in-person setting, a provider can provide certain direct life sustaining care in the event of an emergency, and typically has clear protocols and transfer arrangements in place to get a patient to an emergency department or other acute care setting if necessary. In a telehealth encounter, a provider may not have access to a patient's vitals or other data that might indicate the patient is in need of urgent care. Moreover, if a provider does determine a patient requires emergency care, the provider may not know enough about the patient's location or service area to direct the patient to an appropriate emergency department or urgent care facility. If a patient loses consciousness or otherwise becomes non-responsive during a telehealth encounter, the provider may likewise be unable to identify the patient's location for purposes of notifying emergency responders.

In addressing the issue of emergency care, the Federation of State Medical Boards model policy provides the following:

> An emergency plan is required and must be provided by the physician to the patient when the care provided using telemedicine technologies indicates that a referral to an acute care facility or ER for treatment is necessary for the safety of the patient. The emergency plan should include a formal, written protocol appropriate to the services being rendered via telemedicine technologies.[81]

The American Medical Association takes a similar position, stating merely that "physicians, health professionals and entities that deliver telemedicine services must establish protocols for referrals for emergency services."[82]

Many states have included similar generalized statements. Some, however, have issued more definitive requirements. For example, Colorado Medical Board guidelines for telemedicine require a provider to actually provide an emergency plan to the patient when a referral to an acute care facility or emergency department is necessary for the safety of the patient.[83]

Ultimately, providers may be able to reduce their liability exposure and better serve patients by having specific protocols and procedures for dealing with emergencies in the context of a telehealth encounter as well as appropriate, plain-language disclaimers around this issue for patients receiving telehealth services.

2.7.2 Coordination of Care and Follow-Up

States' requirements relating to coordination of care and follow-up, if any, are fairly general, and leave a fair amount of discretion to providers in how to implement policies and procedures to ensure coordination of care.

Some states, such as California[84] and Colorado, simply tie the issue to the standard of care, requiring physicians to adhere to generally accepted standards relating to continuity and coordina-

---

[81] Fed. State Med. Bds., *supra*, note 79.

[82] American Medical Association, *supra*, note 80.

[83] *See* Colo. Med. Bd., Policy 40-27: Guidelines for the Appropriate Use of Telehealth Technologies in the Practice of Medicine (Aug. 20, 2015).

[84] *See* Cal. Telehealth Advancement Act of 2011.

tion of care.[85] In a few cases, states have established more specific requirements related to follow-up care. For example, as part of its rules relating to prescribing, Alaska effectively requires that follow-up care be available to a patient receiving a prescription based upon a telehealth encounter and that the patient have consented to the prescribing physician sending a copy of all records relating to the encounter to the patient's primary care provider (and such records are sent).[86] In Connecticut, telehealth providers must ask a patient at the time of each telehealth encounter whether the patient consents to the telehealth provider disclosing records regarding the telehealth encounter to the patient's primary care provider and if the patient consents, must provide the records in a timely manner.[87]

The Federation of State Medical Boards has advised as follows with respect to follow-up care:

> Patients should be able to seek, with relative ease, follow-up care or information from the physician [or physician's designee] who conducts an encounter using telemedicine technologies. Physicians solely providing services using telemedicine technologies with no existing physician-patient relationship prior to the encounter must make documentation of the encounter using telemedicine technologies easily available to the patient, and subject to the patient's consent, any identified care provider of the patient immediately after the encounter.[88]

The American Medical Association takes a more specific position on this topic, recommending the following:

> The provision of telemedicine services must include care coordination with the patient's medical home and/or existing treating physicians, which includes at a minimum identifying the patient's existing medical home and treating physician(s) and providing to the latter a copy of the medical record"[89]

Specific protocols and procedures for dealing with specialty referrals, coordination with primary care providers and other issues related to continuity of care may help providers ensure better outcomes for patients and reduced liability exposure for providers.

---

[85] *Id.*

[86] *See* Alaska Stat. § 08.64.364.

[87] *Supra*, note 42, § 19a-906(a)(11).

[88] Fed. State Med. Bds., *supra*, note 79.

[89] American Medical Association, *supra*, note 80.

Chapter 3

Payment and Reimbursement

3.1 Introduction

Coverage, payment, and reimbursement of telehealth services is an area of particularly rapid change—and confusion—among providers. While providers may be familiar with coverage rules for traditional in-person services, the nature of telehealth services renders the landscape notably different. This chapter addresses telehealth payment and reimbursement rules under the Medicare program and state Medicaid programs. It explains the emerging state laws known as telehealth commercial insurance coverage and payment parity statutes. Finally, it concludes with a 50-state survey of state telehealth commercial insurance coverage laws.

3.2 Medicare Coverage of Telehealth Services

Medicare covers certain telehealth services, but the current opportunities are limited, with the coverage restrictions established via statute under the Social Security Act.[1] As the coverage restrictions are statutory in nature, any notable expansion of telehealth coverage under Medicare would require legislation by Congress.

In general, there are five conditions of coverage for telehealth services under Medicare:

1. The beneficiary is located in a qualifying rural area;
2. The beneficiary is located at one of eight qualifying "originating sites;"
3. The services are provided by one of ten "distant site practitioners" eligible to furnish and receive Medicare payment for telehealth services;
4. The beneficiary and distant site practitioner communicate via an interactive audio and video telecommunications system that permits real-time communication between them; and
5. The CPT/HCPCS (Current Procedural Terminology/Healthcare Common Procedure Coding System) code for the service itself is named on the CY2017 (or current year) list of covered Medicare telehealth services.

In order to bill Medicare for telehealth services, the practitioner must fully comply with each of these requirements.[2] If the service does not meet each of these above requirements, the Medicare program will not pay for the service.[3] If the conditions of coverage are met, the use of an interactive telecommunications system substitutes for an in-person encounter (*i.e.*, it satisfies the "face-to-face" element of a service).

3.3 Qualifying Rural Area

The first requirement for coverage is that the patient is located in a rural Health Care Professional Shortage Area (HPSA) outside a Metropolitan Statistical Area (MSA) or in a rural census tract or

---

[1] *See* § 1834(m)(4) of the Social Security Act.

[2] *See* CMS' MLN "Telehealth Services" for CY 2017 ICN 901705 (Nov. 2016).

[3] *See* Section 1834(m)(4)(F) of the Social Security Act; 42 CFR 410.78(f); CMS Pub. 100-02, Medicare Benefit Policy Manual, Ch. 15 section 270.2; CMS Pub. 100-04, Medicare Claims Processing Manual, Ch. 12 section 190.3.

county outside of a MSA. This effectively renders facilities located in urban areas unable to qualify as an originating site and therefore ineligible to enjoy Medicare coverage of telehealth services. Entities participating in a Federal telehealth demonstration project approved by or receiving funding from the Secretary of Health and Human Services as of December 31, 2000, can qualify as originating sites regardless of their geographic location.[4] Such entities are not required to be in a rural HPSA or non MSA. Each year, the geographic eligibility of an originating site is established based on the status of the area as of December 31st of the prior year. Such eligibility continues for the full year.[5]

Recognizing the confusion this restriction has generated, HHS created the "Medicare Telehealth Payment Eligibility Analyzer," a website where a beneficiary or provider can enter a zip code and determine whether or not the geographic location is eligible for Medicare coverage of telehealth services.[6]

3.4 Qualifying Originating Site

The second requirement for coverage is that the patient is located at one of eight qualifying originating sites at the time the service is furnished via a telecommunications system. Medicare beneficiaries are eligible for telehealth services only if the beneficiary is located at one of the following originating sites:

- Office of a Physician or Practitioner;
- Hospital;
- Critical Access Hospital;
- Community Mental Health Center;
- Skilled Nursing Facility;
- Rural Health Clinic;
- Federally Qualified Health Center; and
- Hospital-Based or Critical Access Hospital (CAH)-Based Renal Dialysis Center (including satellites). (Independent Renal Dialysis Facilities are not eligible originating sites).[7]

If a beneficiary receives telehealth services while located at his or her home, those telehealth services will not be covered by Medicare.[8] Many patients choose telehealth services for the convenience and access it offers as an alternative to driving to a practitioner's office and sitting in the waiting room. Accordingly, many telehealth offerings are built around making the services available to patients "on-demand" from their home or workplace during "off hours" for facilities. These services would not be covered by Medicare.

---

[4] *See* CMS' MLN "Telehealth Services" for CY 2017 ICN 901705 (Nov. 2016).

[5] *Id.*

[6] Available at http://datawarehouse.hrsa.gov/tools/analyzers/geo/Telehealth.aspx.

[7] *See* CMS' MLN "Telehealth Services" for CY 2017 ICN 901705 (Nov. 2016).

[8] *Id.*; *see also*, *e.g.*, Noridian Telehealth Services Q&A No. 6 (rev. May 29, 2015) (noting that POS Code 12: home is ineligible for payment).

3.5 Eligible Distant Site Practitioners

The third requirement for coverage is that the services must be provided by a practitioner eligible to furnish telehealth services. Eligible distant site practitioners include:

- Physicians;
- Nurse practitioners;
- Physician assistants;
- Nurse-midwives;
- Clinical nurse specialists;
- Certified registered nurse anesthetists;
- Clinical psychologists;
- Clinical social workers;
- Registered dietitians; and
- Nutrition professionals.[9]

This list of ten eligible practitioners is defined by statute.[10] If a beneficiary receives telehealth services from a practitioner other than those listed above, the service is not covered by Medicare. Although patients receive telehealth services from other practitioners (e.g., RNs, occupational therapists, physical therapists), such telehealth services are not covered by Medicare.

3.6 Eligible Telecommunications Technology

The fourth requirement for coverage is that the beneficiary and distant site practitioner use an interactive audio and video telecommunications system that permits real-time communication.[11] CMS states, "As a condition of payment, you must use an interactive audio and video telecommunications system that permits real-time communication between you, at the distant site, and the beneficiary, at the originating site."[12] This means the practitioner may not use audio-only, store and forward, or other message-based communications if the services are to be covered by Medicare as a telehealth service. There is a limited exception allowing use of asynchronous store and forward technology in Federal telehealth demonstration programs in Alaska or Hawaii.[13]

3.7 Eligible CPT/HCPCS Codes

Finally, the fifth requirement for coverage is that the service itself must be listed among the eligible CPT/HCPCS codes CMS publishes each year as covered telehealth services.[14] In CY 2017, approximately 45 services were covered (with approximately 87 associated codes). Unless a service is listed among the approved codes for telehealth services, Medicare will not cover the service if provided via telehealth.[15]

The result of Medicare's restrictive telehealth laws has been narrow coverage and few claims submitted. For example, in CY 2015, Medicare paid a total of $17.6 million for telehealth service

---

[9] *See* CMS' MLN "Telehealth Services" for CY 2017 ICN 901705 (Nov. 2016).

[10] *See* Section 1834(m)(4)(E) of the Social Security Act.

[11] *See* 42 CFR 410.78(a)(3).

[12] *See* CMS' MLN "Telehealth Services" for CY 2017 ICN 901705 (Nov. 2016).

[13] *Id.*

[14] *Id.*

[15] *Id.*; *see also* www.cms.gov/Medicare/Medicare-General-Information/Telehealth/Telehealth-Codes.html.

claims, compared to an overall $600 billion Medicare program budget.[16] See Figure 3.1. At the same time, patient demand for the convenience and access to care offered by telehealth services has created a willingness for patients (including Medicare beneficiaries) to self-pay out of pocket to enjoy the benefits of these new technologies. Note: coverage rules for Medicare Advantage plans and Medicaid Managed Care organizations are more flexible than traditional fee-for-service Medicare. These plans are encouraged to develop new and innovative ways to provide care, and are generally subject to fewer restrictions on coverage for telehealth services.

Figure 3.1: Medicare Claims for Telehealth Services

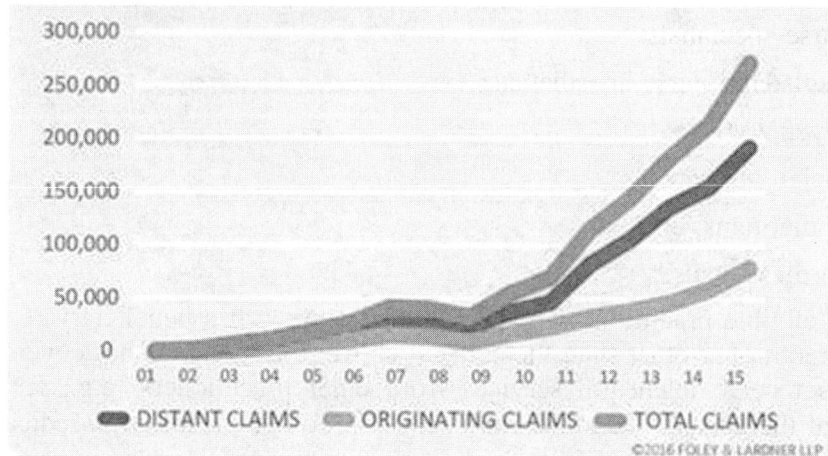

Figure 3.2: Medicare Payments for Telehealth Services

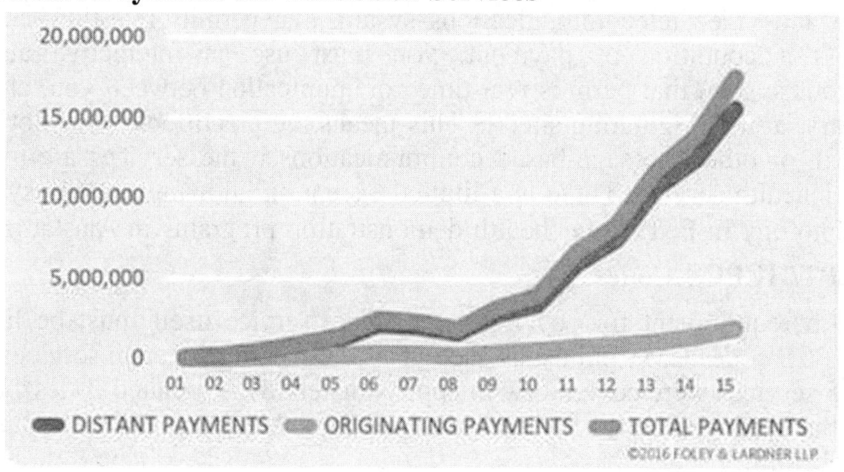

3.8 Medicare Billing, Coding, and Payment for Telehealth Services

CMS has special billing and coding rules for telehealth services under Medicare. Distant site practitioners are instructed to submit claims for telehealth services using the appropriate CPT or HCPCS code for the professional service along with the telehealth modifier GT (meaning "via interactive audio and video telecommunications systems").[17] By coding and billing with the GT modifier for a covered telehealth procedure code, the practitioner certifies that the beneficiary was

---

[16] "Medicare Payments for Telehealth Increased 25% in 2015: What You Need to Know," *Health Care Law Today* (Mar 3, 2016).

[17] *See* CMS' MLN "Telehealth Services" for CY 2017 ICN 901705 (Nov. 2016).

present at an eligible originating site when he or she furnished the telehealth service.[18] By coding and billing with the GT modifier for a covered ESRD-related telehealth service, the practitioner certifies that he or she furnished one "hands on" visit per month to examine the vascular access site.[19]

For Federal telemedicine demonstration programs in Alaska or Hawaii, the distant site practitioner should submit claims using the appropriate CPT or HCPCS code for the professional service along with the telehealth modifier GQ if he/she performed telehealth services "via an asynchronous telecommunications system."[20] By coding and billing with the GQ modifier, the practitioner certifies that the asynchronous medical file was collected and transmitted to him/her at the distant site from a Federal telemedicine demonstration project conducted in Alaska or Hawaii.[21]

In the past, CMS instructed distant site practitioners billing telehealth services to report the Place of Service (POS) Code that would have been reported had the service been furnished in-person where the beneficiary is located (i.e., the originating site). CMS believed that rule generated confusion because some practitioners incorrectly reported the POS where they, themselves, were located when the service is furnished (i.e., the distant site).

Effective January 1, 2017, CMS now instructs practitioners to report a new "telehealth" POS Code "02" to indicate the service was a telehealth service furnished from a distant site.[22] Practitioners must append the GT modifier to the claim, in addition to POS 02.[23] CMS is considering eliminating the GT modifier in future rulemaking, in light of the new POS Code 02 (which itself constitutes a certification that all the statutory telehealth requirements for payment have been met).[24] The telehealth POS code does not apply to originating sites billing the facility fee.[25] CMS reasoned that originating sites are not furnishing a telehealth service as the patient is physically present at the originating site.[26] Accordingly, when billing the originating site fee, the originating site would continue to use the POS code that applies to the type of facility where the patient is located.[27]

Regarding where to submit claims, CMS instructs providers to bill their Medicare Administrative Contractor (MAC) for covered telehealth services.[28] Medicare reimburses providers at the rate set forth in the Physician Fee Schedule.[29] When a provider is located in a Critical Access Hospital (CAH) and has reassigned his/her billing rights to a CAH that elected the Optional Payment Method, the CAH bills the MAC for telehealth services and the payment amount is 80 percent of the Medicare Physician Fee Schedule for telehealth services.[30]

---

[18] *Id.*

[19] *Id.*

[20] *Id.*

[21] *Id.*

[22] *See* MLN Matters MM9726 / CR 9726 (Aug. 12, 2016).

[23] *Id.*

[24] 81 FR 80170, 80199-80201 (Nov. 15, 2016).

[25] *Id.*

[26] *Id.*

[27] *Id.*

[28] *See* CMS' MLN "Telehealth Services" for CY 2017 ICN 901705 (Nov. 2016).

[29] *Id.*

[30] *Id.*

Originating sites are paid an originating site facility fee for telehealth services as described by HCPCS code Q3014.[31] The originating site would bill its MAC for the originating site facility fee, which is a separately billable Part B payment.[32] The current rate is approximately $25.

3.9 Medicare and Other Remote Practitioner Services

Medicare also covers a number of Part B services in which the practitioner and patient have no in-person contact, but which are not considered "telehealth services" for purposes of coverage and billing. A common example would be the remote interpretation of diagnostic tests or images (e.g., MRIs) where the interpreting practitioner is located in a site different from the patient. A medical group could, for example, enter into a contract with a radiologist to provide these interpretive services where the patient is located at the group's Miami center and the radiologist is located at his/her home office in Tampa. These are not considered telehealth services by Medicare and do require the GT modifier. The AMA CPT Codebook also categorizes certain services as "non-face-to-face services" and include such activities as telephone consultations, and electronic or online consultations. Medicare coverage and payment for remote or non-face-to-face services varies and should be assessed under the facts of the particular service or arrangement.

3.10 Medicaid Coverage of Telehealth Services

Reimbursement for Medicaid covered services, including those provided via telehealth, must satisfy federal requirements for efficiency, economy and quality of care.[33] States are encouraged to use the flexibility inherent in federal law to create innovative payment methodologies for services that incorporate telehealth technology.[34] For example, states may pay a physician or other licensed practitioner at the distant site and as well as a facility fee to the originating site.[35] States also can reimburse any additional costs such as technical support, transmission charges, and equipment.[36] These add-on costs can be incorporated into the fee-for-service rates or separately reimbursed as an administrative cost by the state.[37] If they are separately billed and reimbursed, the costs must be linked to a covered Medicaid service.[38]

Actual Medicaid coverage of telehealth services varies significantly across states, but every state Medicaid program offers some coverage of telehealth services. Highlights include the following:

- 50 state Medicaid programs offer some type of coverage for telehealth services (most commonly interactive live video).[39]
- 9 state Medicaid programs offer coverage of asynchronous (store-and-forward) telehealth services, not including states that only cover teleradiology.
- 29 state Medicaid programs offer coverage of telehealth-based home health services, which may sometimes include remote patient monitoring technologies.
- 30 state Medicaid programs pay an additional transmission or facility fee when telehealth is

[31] *Id.*

[32] *Id.*

[33] *See* www.medicaid.gov/medicaid/benefits/telemed/index.html.

[34] *Id.*

[35] *Id.*

[36] *Id.*

[37] *Id.*

[38] *Id.*

[39] American Telemedicine Association, Feb. 2017, *State Telemedicine Gaps Analysis: Coverage & Reimbursement*. Washington, DC.

used.

- 47 state Medicaid programs offer coverage without geographic restrictions (e.g., rural or urban).
- 40 state Medicaid programs allow the patient's home to serve as an originating site.

In addition to the varied and continually-changing nature of Medicaid telehealth coverage, some state Medicaid coverage rules are derived from multiple sources, including state regulations, state plan amendments (SPA), Medicaid provider handbooks or manuals, Medicaid all-provider letters, and the like. Some states, like Florida, have employed a clear, streamlined approach. For example, Florida's Medicaid telehealth coverage rule states:

> (1) This rule applies to any person or entity prescribing or reviewing a request for Florida Medicaid services and to all providers of Florida Medicaid services that are enrolled in or registered with the Florida Medicaid program.
>
> (2) **Definition**. Telemedicine—The practice of health care delivery by a practitioner who is located at a site other than the site where a recipient is located for the purposes of evaluation, diagnosis, or treatment.
>
> (3) **Who Can Provide**. Practitioners licensed within their scope of practice to perform the service.
>
> (4) **Coverage**. Florida Medicaid reimburses for telemedicine services using interactive telecommunications equipment that includes, at a minimum audio and video equipment permitting two-way, real time, interactive communication between a recipient and a practitioner.
>
> (5) **Exclusion**. Florida Medicaid does not reimburse for:
>
> (a) Telephone conversations, chart review(s), electronic mail messages, or facsimile transmissions.
>
> (b) Equipment required to provide telemedicine services.
>
> (6) **Reimbursement**. The following applies to practitioners rendering services in the fee-for-service delivery system:
>
> (a) Florida Medicaid reimburses the practitioner who is providing the evaluation, diagnosis, or treatment recommendation located at a site other than where the recipient is located.
>
> (b) Providers must include modifier GT on the CMS-1500 claim form, incorporated by reference in Rule 59G-4.001, F.A.C.[40]

States are not required to submit a (separate) SPA for coverage or reimbursement of telehealth services if they decide to reimburse for telehealth services the same way/amount that they pay for face-to-face services.[41] States must submit a (separate) reimbursement SPA if they want to provide reimbursement for telehealth services or components of telehealth differently than is currently being reimbursed for face-to-face services.[42] States may submit a coverage SPA to better describe the telehealth services they choose to cover, such as which providers/practitioners are covered; where the service may be provided; how it may be provided, etc.[43] In that event, and in order to avoid unnecessary SPA submissions, CMS recommends that a brief description of the framework for telehealth coverage be placed in an introductory section of the State Plan, with a reference to

---

[40] *See* Fla. Admin. Code r. 59G-1.057.

[41] *See* www.medicaid.gov/medicaid/benefits/telemed/index.html.

[42] *Id.*

[43] *Id.*

telehealth coverage in the applicable benefit sections of the State Plan.[44] For example, in the physician section it might say that dermatology services can be delivered via telehealth provided all state requirements related to telehealth as described in the State Plan are otherwise met.[45]

3.11 Commercial Telehealth Insurance Coverage Laws

3.11.1 Telehealth Commercial Coverage Laws

Thirty-one states and the District of Columbia have enacted telehealth commercial insurance coverage laws, with bills currently under development in several other states. See Figure 3.3. These laws generally are referred to as telehealth commercial payer statutes or telehealth parity laws. They are designed to promote patient access to care via telehealth, whether the patient is in a rural area without specialist care or a busy metropolitan city without the time to leave work or the home to devote three or more hours to an in-person check-up in a crowded waiting room. There are significant variances across the states, but two related but distinct concepts have emerged: telehealth coverage and telehealth payment parity.

Telehealth coverage laws require health plans to cover services provided via telehealth to the same extent the plan already covers the services if provided through an in-person visit. The laws do not mandate the health plan provide entirely new service lines or specialties, and the scope of services in the enrollee's member benefit package remains unchanged. The only difference is that the patient can choose to see his or her doctor via telehealth rather than be compelled to drive to the doctor's waiting room for an in-person consult.

Telehealth coverage laws also frequently include language to protect patients from cost-shifting. This language disallows health plans from imposing different deductibles, co-payments, or maximum benefit caps for services provided via telehealth. Any deductibles, co-payments and benefit caps apply equally and identically whether the patient receives the care in-person or via telehealth. This prevents the patient from being saddled with higher co-payments to access care via telehealth.

Some states, particularly those that have enacted telehealth coverage laws in the last few years, have elected to expand on telehealth coverage by also requiring health plans to cover remote patient monitoring. Remote patient monitoring includes a variety of patient oversight and communications devices, software, and processes to allow providers a greater ability to monitor patient care needs and immediately respond. States have taken this step because remote patient monitoring, by definition, is a virtual distance-based service and does not have an in-person equivalent that would likely already be found in a member's benefit package.

The following states have enacted telehealth commercial insurance coverage laws:

Figure 3.3: States with Telehealth Commercial Insurance Coverage Laws

Alaska	**Delaware**	**Maryland**	**New Hampshire**	**Texas**
Arizona	**Georgia**	**Michigan**	**New Mexico**	**Vermont**
Arkansas	**Hawaii**	**Minnesota**	**New York**	**Virginia**
California	**Indiana**	**Mississippi**	**Oklahoma**	**Washington**
Colorado	**Kentucky**	**Missouri**	**Oregon**	
Connecticut	**Louisiana**	**Montana**	**Rhode Island**	
D.C.	**Maine**	**Nevada**	**Tennessee**	

[44] *Id.*

[45] *Id.*

3.11.2 Telehealth Payment Parity Laws

A subset of states include payment parity language in their telehealth commercial insurance coverage laws. Telehealth payment parity is different from coverage. Telehealth payment parity enables providers for telehealth services to be reimbursed at the same or equivalent rate the health plan pays the provider when the service is provided in-person. For example, assume a doctor's participation agreement with a health plan reimburses the doctor $100 for a patient exam. Under a telehealth payment parity law, the health plan pays the doctor $100 whether he provides the service in-person or via telehealth, so long as the doctor does not agree to accept a lower rate (or alternative payment model) for services provided via telehealth under the participation agreement. If the agreed-upon contract rate is $30 for the in-person service, it is also typically $30 for telehealth. Payment parity does not change the plan's existing utilization review processes. The doctor's services (whether in-person or via telehealth) must still be of high quality, appropriately documented, and medically necessary in order to be paid.

Payment parity is intended to level the field for providers to enter into meaningful negotiations with health plans as to how telehealth services are covered and paid. Payment parity does not eliminate opportunities for cost savings, as plans and providers may still voluntarily contract for alternative payment models and compensation methodologies. Nor are payment parity laws intended to prohibit health plans and providers from the freedom to develop and enter into at-risk, capitated or shared savings contracts, all of which are conducive to the benefits offered by telehealth.

3.11.3 Consequences of a Telehealth Coverage Law without Payment Parity

Payment parity is, in part, a response to avoid health plans paying for telehealth services at only a percentage of the in-person rate. This situation currently exists in many states that enacted a telehealth coverage statute but failed to include payment parity language. If the health plan's payment rate is too low, it can create a disincentive for providers to offer telehealth services and contravene the very policy purposes underpinning the law itself.

This very thing occurred in New York. After New York's coverage law became effective in January 2016, some health plans announced they would cover telehealth-based services as required, but would pay at only 50% of the reimbursement rate for identical in-person services. This was met with significant upset in the provider community, particularly by in-network providers as they were no longer able to offer their patients the choice of paying out-of-pocket for telehealth services. These providers either had to accept the 50% payment or elect to discontinue offering telehealth services. Legislation was introduced a few months later to add payment parity to the telehealth law, and have health plans "reimburse a telehealth provider for covered services delivered via telehealth on the same basis and at the same rate as established for the same service when not delivered via telehealth."[46] Such consequences (unintended or otherwise) should be thoughtfully considered and discussed when a state legislature evaluates a telehealth insurance coverage bill.

3.11.4 How Differences in Telehealth Insurance Laws Affect Patients and the Marketplace

For a state to promote meaningful adoption of telehealth, much depends on the language of its statute. A narrowly drawn statute may provide coverage only for telemedicine and define it as licensed physician services. In that event, the telehealth market will see growth primarily in physician consults and other physician-driven health care services.

If, instead, a statute is drafted more broadly to include telehealth, virtual care, and/or remote patient monitoring, the state will see growth in those areas, including equipment manufacturing,

[46] *See* SB 7953 (2016).

software development, and other technologies associated with virtual care services. This could also trigger growth in companies that create patient health apps or data-driven interfaces, all of which are part of the virtual care services enterprise.

When drafting a telehealth commercial insurance coverage law, another important decision point is whether to:

1. Cover telehealth-based services to the same extent that service is covered when provided in-person; or
2. Cover additional telehealth-based services, such as remote patient monitoring and mHealth apps, even if they are not covered in the in-person setting.

Depending on the legislature's goals, different statutory language is appropriate because the certain telehealth services (remote patient monitoring, mHealth), by definition, do not typically exist in the in-person setting. Therefore, they will not often be covered as an in-person benefit.

For example, if the legislature's intent is to cover a broad spectrum of telehealth services, but the bill's language reads "health plans must cover services provided via telehealth to the same extent those services are covered if provided in-person," that bill could create a coverage gap omitting remote patient monitoring because many health plans do not provide coverage for an in-person equivalent to remote patient monitoring. For this reason, some states (e.g., Mississippi) have enacted follow-up legislation to expressly expand the scope of covered telehealth services, even after enacting a first telehealth coverage statute.

Minnesota's telehealth insurance law, for example, includes language for coverage and payment parity. It states, in pertinent part, as follows:

- A health plan [. . .] *shall include* coverage for telemedicine benefits in the same manner as any other benefits covered under the policy, plan, or contract, and shall comply with the regulations of this section.
- A health carrier *shall not exclude* a service for coverage solely because the service is provided via telemedicine and is not provided through in-person consultation or contact between a licensed health care provider and a patient.
- A health carrier shall reimburse the distant site licensed health care provider for covered services delivered via telemedicine *on the same basis and at the same rate* as the health carrier would apply to those services if the services had been delivered in person by the distant site licensed health care provider.
- It is not a violation of this subdivision for a health carrier to include a deductible, co-payment, or coinsurance requirement for a health care service provided via telemedicine, provided that the deductible, co-payment, or coinsurance is not in addition to, and does not exceed, the deductible, co-payment, or coinsurance applicable if the same services were provided through in-person contact.[47]

In contrast, Maine's telehealth insurance coverage law addresses coverage, but not payment parity, stating as follows:

> Coverage of telemedicine services. A carrier offering a health plan in this State may not deny coverage on the basis that the coverage is provided through telemedicine if the health care service would be covered were it provided through in-person consultation between the covered person and a health care provider. Coverage for health care services provided through telemedicine must be determined in a manner consistent with coverage for health care services

[47] *See* MN Stat. 62A.672 (emph. added).

> provided through in-person consultation. A carrier may offer a health plan containing a provision for a deductible, copayment or coinsurance requirement for a health care service provided through telemedicine as long as the deductible, copayment or coinsurance does not exceed the deductible, copayment or coinsurance applicable to an in-person consultation.[48]

As a third point of comparison, Michigan's telehealth insurance law lacks a clear mandate or expectation for coverage and parity, instead deferring significantly to the insurers. It states, in pertinent part, as follows:

> A group or non-group health care corporation certificate shall not require face-to-face contact between a health care professional and a patient for services appropriately provided through telemedicine, *as determined by the health care corporation.* Telemedicine services shall be provided by a health care professional who is licensed, registered, or otherwise authorized to engage in his or her health care profession in the state where the patient is located. Telemedicine services are subject to all terms and conditions of the certificate agreed upon between the certificate holder and the health care corporation, including, but not limited to, required copayments, coinsurances, deductibles and approved amounts.[49]

3.11.5 Language to Consider in a Telehealth Commercial Insurance Statute

When drafting a telehealth coverage bill, lawmakers can consider the following provisions designed to be affirmative in nature, use clear and concise language, and be self-evident within a single sentence.

- **Coverage:** All health insurance plans in this state must provide coverage for health care services delivered via telehealth to the same extent the services would be covered if they were delivered via an in-person encounter.
- **Payment parity:** A health insurance plan shall reimburse for health care services delivered via telehealth on the same basis and at least the same rate that the health insurance plan reimburses for comparable health care services delivered via in-person encounters.
- **Geographic freedom:** A health insurance plan may not impose any originating site restrictions, nor distinguish between patients in rural or urban locations when providing coverage under the policy or contract for health care services delivered via telehealth.
- **Narrow networking:** A health insurance plan may not limit coverage of telehealth services only to those health care providers who are members of the insurance plan's provider network.
- **Patient co-payments:** A health insurance plan may charge a deductible, co-payment, or coinsurance for a health care service provided through telemedicine so long as it does not exceed the deductible, co-payment, or coinsurance applicable to an in-person consultation.
- **Patient lifetime benefit:** A health insurance plan may impose any annual or lifetime dollar maximum on coverage for telemedicine services other than an annual or lifetime dollar maximum that applies in the aggregate to all items and services covered under the policy, or impose upon any person receiving benefits pursuant to this section any copayment, coinsurance, or deductible amounts, or any policy year, calendar year, lifetime, or other durational benefit limitation or maximum for benefits or services, that is not equally imposed upon all terms and services covered under the policy, contract, or plan.

---

[48] *See* 24-A M.R.S.A. § 4316(2).

[49] *See* MI Stat. § 550.1401k(1) (emph. added).

Table 3.1 50-State Survey: Telehealth Commercial Insurance Coverage Laws

ALABAMA

(NONE)

ALASKA

Alaska Stat. 21.42.422

Coverage for telehealth and mental health benefits

A health care insurer that offers, issues for delivery, or renews in the state a health care insurance plan in the group or individual market that provides mental health benefits shall provide coverage for mental health benefits provided through telehealth by a health care provider licensed in the state and may not require that prior in-person contact occur between a health care provider and a patient before payment is made for covered services.

ARIZONA

ARS 20-841.09

Telemedicine; coverage of health care services; definitions

A. All contracts issued, delivered or renewed on or after January 1, 2015 must provide coverage for health care services that are provided through telemedicine if the health care service would be covered were it provided through in-person consultation between the subscriber and a health care provider; and provided to a subscriber receiving the service in a rural region of this state. The contract may limit the coverage to those health care providers who are members of the corporation's provider network.

B. This section does not prevent a corporation from imposing deductibles, copayment or coinsurance requirements for a health care service provided through telemedicine if the deductible, copayment or coinsurance does not exceed the deductible, copayment or coinsurance applicable to an in-person consultation for the same health care service.

C. Services provided through telemedicine or resulting from a telemedicine consultation shall comply with Arizona licensure requirements, accreditation standards and any practice guidelines of a national association of medical professionals promoting access to medical care for consumers via telecommunications technology or other qualified medical professional societies to ensure quality of care.

D. This section does not apply to limited benefit coverage as defined in section 20-1137.

E. For the purposes of this section:

1. "Health care services" means services provided for the following conditions or in the following settings:

(a) Trauma.

(b) Burn.

(c) Cardiology.

(d) Infectious diseases.

(e) Mental health disorders.

(f) Neurologic diseases including strokes.

(g) Dermatology.

2. "Rural region" means either:

(a) An area that is located in a county with a population of less than nine hundred thousand persons; or

(b) A city or town that is located in a county with a population of nine hundred thousand persons or more, and whose nearest boundary is more than thirty miles from the boundary of a city that has a population of five hundred thousand persons or more.

3. "Telemedicine":

(a) Means the interactive use of audio, video or other electronic media for the purpose of diagnosis, consultation or treatment.

(b) Does not include the sole use of an audio-only telephone, a video-only system, a facsimile machine, instant messages or electronic mail.

ARKANSAS

ACA 23-79-1601

Definitions

As used in this subchapter:

(1) "Distant site" means the location of the health care professional delivering health care services through telemedicine at the time the services are provided;

(2) (A) "Health benefit plan" means:

(i) An individual, blanket or group plan, policy or contract for health care services issued or delivered by an insurer, health maintenance organization, hospital medical service corporation or self-insured governmental or church plan in this state; and

(ii) Any health benefit program receiving state or federal appropriations from the State of Arkansas, including the Arkansas Medicaid Program and the Health Care Independence Program, commonly referred to as the "Private Option," or any successor program.

(B) "Health benefit plan" includes:

(i) Indemnity and managed care plans; and

(ii) Nonfederal governmental plans as defined in 29 U.S.C. § 1002(32), as it existed on January 1, 2015.

(C) "Health benefit plan" does not include:

(i) Disability income plans;

(ii) Credit insurance plans;

(iii) Insurance coverage issued as a supplement to liability insurance;

(iv) Medical payments under automobile or homeowners insurance plans;

(v) Health benefit plans provided under Arkansas Constitution, Article 5, § 32, the Workers' Compensation Law, § 11-9-101 *et seq.*, or the Public Employee Workers' Compensation Act, § 21-5-601 *et seq.*;

(vi) Plans that provide only indemnity for hospital confinement;

(vii) Accident only plans;

(viii) Specified disease plans; or

(ix) Long-term care only plans;

(3) "Health care professional" means a person who is licensed, certified, or otherwise authorized by the laws of this state to administer health care in the ordinary course of the practice of his or her profession;

(4) "Originating site" means:

(A) The offices of a health care professional or a licensed health care entity where the patient is located at the time services are provided by a health care professional through telemedicine; and

(B) The home of a patient in connection with treatment for end-stage renal disease; and

(5) "Telemedicine" means the medium of delivering clinical health care services by means of real-time two-way electronic audio-visual communications, including without limitation, the application of secure video conferencing, to provide or support health care delivery that facilitates the assessment, diagnosis, consultation or treatment of a patient's health care while the patient is at an originating site and the health care professional is at a distant site.

ACA 23-79-1602

Coverage for telemedicine

(a) (1) This subchapter shall apply to all health benefit plans delivered, issued for delivery, reissued, or extended in Arkansas on or after January 1, 2016, or at any time when any term of the health benefit plan is changed or any premium adjustment is made thereafter.

(2) Notwithstanding subdivision (a)(1) of this section, this subchapter shall apply to the Arkansas Medicaid Program on and after July 1, 2016.

(b) A health care service provided through telemedicine shall comply with the requirements of § 17-80-117.

(c) (1) A health benefit plan shall cover the services of a physician who is licensed by the Arkansas State Medical Board for health care services through telemedicine on the same basis as the health benefit plan provides coverage for the same health care services provided by the physician in person.

(2) Subject to subdivision (d)(1) of this section, a health benefit plan shall reimburse a physician licensed by the board for health care services provided through telemedicine on the same basis as the health benefit plan reimburses a physician for the same health care services provided in person.

(d) (1) The combined amount of reimbursement that a health benefit plan allows for the compensation to the distant site physician and the originating site shall not be less than the total amount allowed for health care services provided in person.

(2) Payment for health care services provided through telemedicine shall be provided to the distant site physician and the originating site upon submission of the appropriate procedure codes.

(3) This section does not:

(A) Prohibit:

(i) A health benefit plan from reimbursing other health care professionals; or

(ii) A health benefit plan from paying a facility fee to a provider at the distant site in addition to a fee paid to the health care professional; or

(B) Require an insurer to pay more for a health care service provided through telemedicine than would have been paid if the health care service was delivered in person.

(e) A health benefit plan shall not impose on coverage for health care services provided through telemedicine:

(1) An annual or lifetime dollar maximum on coverage for services provided through telemedicine other than an annual or lifetime dollar maximum that applies to the aggregate of all items and services covered;

(2) A deductible, copayment, coinsurance, benefit limitation or maximum benefit that is not equally imposed upon all health care services covered under the health benefit plan; or

(3) A prior authorization requirement for services provided through telemedicine that exceeds the prior authorization requirement for in-person health care services under the health benefit plan.

(f) This subchapter does not prohibit a health benefit plan from:

(1) Limiting coverage of health care services provided through telemedicine to medically necessary services, subject to the same terms and conditions of the covered person's health benefit plan that apply to services provided in person; or

(2) (A) Undertaking utilization review, including prior authorization, to determine the appropriateness of health care services provided through telemedicine, provided that:

(i) The determination of appropriateness is made in the same manner as determinations are made for the treatment of any illness, condition or disorder covered by the health benefit plan whether the service was provided in-person or through telemedicine; and

(ii) All adverse determinations are made by a physician who possesses a current and valid unrestricted license to practice medicine in Arkansas.

(B) Utilization review shall not require prior authorization of emergent telemedicine services.

(g) (1) A health benefit plan may adopt policies to ensure that health care services provided through telemedicine submitted for payment comply with the same coding, documentation and other requirements necessary for payment as an in-person service other than the in-person requirement.

(2) If deemed necessary, the State Insurance Department may promulgate rules containing additional standards and procedures for the utilization of telemedicine to provide health care service through health benefit plans if the additional standards and procedures do not conflict with this subchapter or § 17-80-117 and are applied uniformly by all health benefit plans.

CALIFORNIA

Health & Safety Code 1374.13

(a) For the purposes of this section, the definitions in subdivision (a) of Section 2290.5 of the Business and Professions Code shall apply.

(b) It is the intent of the Legislature to recognize the practice of telehealth as a legitimate means by which an individual may receive health care services from a health care provider without in-person contact with the health care provider.

(c) No health care service plan shall require that in-person contact occur between a health care provider and a patient before payment is made for the covered services appropriately provided through telehealth, subject to the terms and conditions of the contract entered into between the enrollee or subscriber and the health care service plan, and between the health care service plan and its participating providers or provider groups.

(d) No health care service plan shall limit the type of setting where services are provided for the patient or by the health care provider before payment is made for the covered services appropriately provided through telehealth, subject to the terms and conditions of the contract entered into between the enrollee or subscriber and the health care service plan, and between the health care service plan and its participating providers or provider groups.

(e) The requirements of this section shall also apply to health care service plan and Medi-Cal managed care plan contracts with the State Department of Health Care Services pursuant to Chapter 7 (commencing with Section 14000) or Chapter 8 (commencing with Section 14200) of Part 3 of Division 9 of the Welfare and Institutions Code.

(f) Notwithstanding any other provision, this section shall not be interpreted to authorize a health care service plan to require the use of telehealth when the health care provider has determined that it is not appropriate.

COLORADO

CO Stat. 10-16-123

Telehealth

(1) It is the intent of the general assembly to recognize the practice of telehealth as a legitimate means by which an individual may receive health care services from a provider without in-person contact with the provider.

(2) (a) On or after January 1, 2017, a health benefit plan that is issued, amended or renewed in this state shall not require in-person contact between a provider and a covered person for services appropriately provided through telehealth, subject to all terms and conditions of the health benefit plan. Nothing in this section requires the use of telehealth when a provider determines that delivery of care through telehealth is not appropriate or when a covered person chooses not to receive care through telehealth. A provider is not obligated to document or demonstrate that a barrier to in-person care exists to trigger coverage under a health benefit plan for services provided through telehealth.

(b) Subject to all terms and conditions of the health benefit plan, a carrier shall reimburse the treating participating provider or the consulting participating provider for the diagnosis, consultation or treatment of the covered person delivered through telehealth on the same basis that the carrier is responsible for reimbursing that provider for the provision of the same service through in-person consultation or contact by that provider. A carrier shall not deny coverage of a health care service that is a covered benefit because the service is provided through telehealth rather than in-person consultation or contact between the participating provider or, subject to section 10-16-704, the nonparticipating provider and the covered person where the health care service is appropriately provided through telehealth. Section 10-16-704 applies to this paragraph (b).

(c) A carrier shall include in the payment for telehealth interactions reasonable compensation to the originating site for the transmission cost incurred during the delivery of health care services through telehealth; except that, for purposes of this paragraph (c), the originating site does not include a private residence at which the covered person is located when he or she receives health care services through telehealth.

(d) A carrier may offer a health coverage plan containing a deductible, copayment or coinsurance requirement for a health care service provided through telehealth, but the deductible, copayment or coinsurance amount must not exceed the deductible, copayment or coinsurance applicable if the same health care services are provided through in-person diagnosis, consultation or treatment.

(e) A carrier shall not impose an annual dollar maximum on coverage for health care services covered under the health benefit plan that are delivered through telehealth, other than an annual dollar maximum that applies to the same services when performed by the same provider through in-person care.

(f) If a covered person receives health care services through telehealth, a carrier shall apply the same copayment, coinsurance or deductible amount and policy-year, calendar-year, lifetime, or other durational benefit limitation or maximum benefits or services under the health benefit plan to the health care services delivered via telehealth that the carrier applies under the health benefit plan to those health care services when performed by the same provider through in-person care.

(g) (I) The requirements of this section apply to all health benefit plans delivered, issued for delivery, amended, or renewed in this state on or after January 1, 2017, or at any time after that date when a term of the plan is changed or a premium adjustment is made.

(II) This section does not apply to:

(A) Short-term travel, accident-only, limited or specified disease, or individual conversion policies or contracts; or

(B) Policies or contracts designed for issuance to persons eligible for coverage under Title XVIII of the "Social Security Act," as amended, or any other similar coverage under state or federal governmental plans.

(h) Nothing in this section prohibits a carrier from providing coverage or reimbursement for health care services appropriately provided through telehealth to a covered person who is not located at an originating site.

(3) A health benefit plan shall not be required to pay for consultation provided by a provider by telephone or facsimile.

(4) As used in this section:

(a) "Distant site" means a site at which a provider is located while providing health care services by means of telehealth.

(b) "Originating site" means a site at which a patient is located at the time health care services are provided to him or her by means of telehealth.

(c) "Store-and-forward transfer" means the electronic transfer of a patient's medical information or an interaction between providers that occurs between an originating site and distant sites when the patient is not present.

(d) "Synchronous interaction" means a real-time interaction between a patient located at the originating site and a provider located at a distant site.

(e) (I) "Telehealth" means a mode of delivery of health care services through telecommunications systems, including information, electronic, and communication technologies, to facilitate the assessment, diagnosis, consultation, treatment, education, care management or self-management of a covered person's health care while the covered person is located at an originating site and the provider is located at a distant site. The term includes synchronous interactions and store-and-forward transfers.

(II) "Telehealth" does not include the delivery of health care services via telephone, facsimile machine, or electronic mail systems.

CONNECTICUT

Public Act No. 15-88

Section 1.

(a) As used in this section:

(1) "Asynchronous" means any transmission to another site for review at a later time that uses a camera or other technology to capture images or data to be recorded.

(2) "Health record" means the record of individual, health-related information that may include, but need not be limited to, continuity of care documents, discharge summaries and other information or data relating to a patient's demographics, medical history, medication, allergies, immunizations, laboratory test results, radiology or other diagnostic images, vital signs and statistics.

(3) "Facility fee" has the same meaning as in section 19a-508c of the general statutes.

(4) "Medical history" means information, including, but not limited to, a patient's past illnesses, medications, hospitalizations, family history of illness if known, the name and address of the patient's primary care provider if known and other matters relating to the health condition of the patient at the time of a telehealth interaction.

(5) "Originating site" means a site at which a patient is located at the time health care services are provided to the patient by means of telehealth.

(6) "Peripheral devices" means the instruments a telehealth provider uses to perform a patient exam, including, but not limited to, stethoscope, otoscope, ophthalmoscope, sphygmomanometer, thermometer, tongue depressor and reflex hammer.

(7) "Remote patient monitoring" means the personal health and medical data collection from a patient in one location via electronic communication technologies that is then transmitted to a telehealth provider located at a distant site for the purpose of health care monitoring to assist the effective management of the patient's treatment, care and related support.

(8) "Store and forward transfer" means the asynchronous transmission of a patient's medical information from an originating site to the telehealth provider at a distant site.

(9) "Synchronous" means real-time interactive technology.

(10) "Telehealth" means the mode of delivering health care or other health services via information and communication technologies to facilitate the diagnosis, consultation and treatment, education, care management and self-management of a patient's physical and mental health, and includes (A) interaction between the patient at the originating site and the telehealth provider at a distant site, and (B) synchronous interactions, asynchronous store and forward transfers or remote patient monitoring. Telehealth does not include the use of facsimile, audio-only telephone, texting or electronic mail.

(11) "Telehealth provider" means any physician licensed under chapter 370 of the general statutes, physical therapist licensed under chapter 376 of the general statutes, chiropractor licensed under chapter 372 of the general statutes, naturopath licensed under chapter 373 of the general statutes, podiatrist licensed under chapter 375 of the general statutes, occupational therapist licensed under chapter 376a of the general statutes, optometrist licensed under chapter 380 of the general statutes, advanced practice registered nurse licensed under chapter 378 of the general statutes, physician assistant licensed under chapter 370 of the general statutes, psychologist licensed under chapter 383 of the general statutes, marital and family therapist licensed under chapter 383a of the general statutes, clinical social worker or master social worker licensed under chapter 383b of the general statutes, alcohol and drug counselor licensed under chapter 376b of the general statutes, professional counselor licensed under chapter 383c of the general statutes or dietitian-nutritionist certified under chapter 384b of the general statutes, who is providing health care or other health services through the use of telehealth within such person's scope of practice and in accordance with the standard of care applicable to the profession.

(b) (1) A telehealth provider shall only provide telehealth services to a patient when the telehealth provider: (A) Is communicating through real-time, interactive, two-way communication technology or store and forward technologies; (B) has access to, or knowledge of, the patient's medical history, as provided by the patient, and the patient's health record, including the name and address of the patient's primary care provider, if any; (C) conforms to the standard of care applicable to the telehealth provider's profession and expected for in-person care as appropriate to the patient's age and presenting condition, except when the standard of care requires the use of diagnostic testing and performance of a physical examination, such testing or examination may be carried out through the use of peripheral devices appropriate to the patient's condition; and (D) provides the patient with the telehealth's provider license number and contact information.

(2) At the time of the telehealth provider's first telehealth interaction with a patient, the telehealth provider shall inform the patient concerning the treatment methods and limitations of treatment using a telehealth platform and, after providing the patient with such information,

obtain the patient's consent to provide telehealth services. The telehealth provider shall document such notice and consent in the patient's health record.

(c) Notwithstanding the provisions of this section or title 20 of the general statutes, no telehealth provider shall prescribe schedule I, II or III controlled substances through the use of telehealth.

(d) Each telehealth provider shall, at the time of each telehealth interaction, ask the patient whether the patient consents to the telehealth's provider disclosure of records concerning the telehealth interaction to the patient's primary care provider. If the patient consents to such disclosure, the telehealth provider shall provide such records to the patient's primary care provider, in a timely manner, in accordance with the provisions of sections 20-7b to 20-7e, inclusive, of the general statutes.

(e) The provision of telehealth services and health records maintained and disclosed as part of a telehealth interaction shall comply with the provisions of the Health Insurance Portability and Accountability Act of 1996 P. L. 104-191, as amended from time to time.

(f) Nothing in this section shall prohibit: (1) A health care provider from providing on-call coverage pursuant to an agreement with another health care provider or such health care provider's professional entity or employer; (2) a health care provider from consulting with another health care provider concerning a patient's care; or (3) orders of health care providers for hospital outpatients or inpatients. For purposes of this subsection, "health care provider" means a person or entity licensed or certified pursuant to chapter 370, 372, 373, 375, 378 or 379 of the general statutes or licensed or certified pursuant to chapter 368d or 384d of the general statutes.

(g) No telehealth provider shall charge a facility fee for telehealth services.

Sec. 2.

(a) As used in this section, "telehealth" has the same meaning provided in section 1 of this act.

(b) Each individual health insurance policy providing coverage of the type specified in subdivisions (1), (2), (4), (11) and (12) of section 38a-469 of the general statutes delivered, issued for delivery, renewed, amended or continued in this state shall provide coverage for medical advice, diagnosis, care or treatment provided through telehealth, to the extent coverage is provided for such advice, diagnosis, care or treatment when provided through in-person consultation between the insured and a health care provider. Such coverage shall be subject to the same terms and conditions applicable to all other benefits under such policy.

(c) No such policy shall: (1) Exclude a service for coverage solely because such service is provided only through telehealth and not through in-person consultation between the insured and a health care provider, provided telehealth is appropriate for the provision of such service; or (2) be required to reimburse a treating or consulting health care provider for the technical fees or technical costs for the provision of telehealth services.

(d) Nothing in this section shall prohibit or limit a health insurer, health care center, hospital service corporation, medical service corporation or other entity from conducting utilization review for telehealth services, provided such utilization review is conducted in the same manner and uses the same clinical review criteria as a utilization review for an in-person consultation for the same service.

Sec. 3.

(a) As used in this section, "telehealth" has the same meaning provided in section 1 of this act.

(b) Each group health insurance policy providing coverage of the type specified in subdivisions (1), (2), (4), (11) and (12) of section 38a-469 of the general statutes delivered, issued for delivery, renewed, amended or continued in this state shall provide coverage for medical advice, diagnosis, care or treatment provided through telehealth, to the extent coverage is provided for such advice, diagnosis, care or treatment when provided through in-person consultation between the insured and a health care provider. Such coverage shall be subject to the same terms and conditions applicable to all other benefits under such policy.

(c) No such policy shall: (1) Exclude a service for coverage solely because such service is provided only through telehealth and not through in-person consultation between the insured and a health care provider, provided telehealth is appropriate for the provision of such service; or (2) be required to reimburse a treating or consulting health care provider for the technical fees or technical costs for the provision of telehealth services.

(d) Nothing in this section shall prohibit or limit a health insurer, health care center, hospital service corporation, medical service corporation or other entity from conducting utilization review for telehealth services, provided such utilization review is conducted in the same manner and uses the same clinical review criteria as a utilization review for an in-person consultation for the same service.

DELAWARE

18 Del Code § 3370

Telemedicine

(a) As used in this section:

(1) "Distant site" means a site at which a health-care provider legally allowed to practice in the State is located while providing health-care services by means of telemedicine or telehealth.

(2) "Originating site" means a site in Delaware at which a patient is located at the time health care services are provided to him or her by means of telemedicine or telehealth, unless the term is otherwise defined with respect to the provision in which it is used; provided, however, notwithstanding any other provision of law, insurers and providers may agree to alternative siting arrangements deemed appropriate by the parties.

(3) "Store and forward transfer" means the transmission of a patient's medical information either to or from an originating site or to or from the provider at the distant site, but does not require the patient being present nor must it be in real time.

(4) "Telehealth" means the use of information and communications technologies consisting of telephones, remote patient monitoring devices or other electronic means which support clinical health care, provider consultation, patient and professional health-related education, public health, health administration, and other services as described in regulation.

(5) "Telemedicine" means a form of telehealth which is the delivery of clinical health care services by means of real time 2-way audio, visual, or other telecommunications or electronic communications, including the application of secure video conferencing or store and forward transfer technology to provide or support health care delivery, which facilitate the assessment, diagnosis, consultation, treatment, education, care management and self-management of a patient's health care by a health-care provider practicing within his or her scope of practice as would be practiced in-person with a patient, and legally allowed to practice in the State, while such patient is at an originating site and the health care provider is at a distant site.

(b) Each insurer proposing to issue individual or group accident and sickness insurance policies providing hospital, medical and surgical, or major medical coverage on an expense-incurred basis; each health service corporation providing individual or group accident and sickness subscription contracts; and each health maintenance organization providing a health care plan for health care services shall provide coverage for the cost of such health care services provided through telemedicine.

(c) Each insurer proposing to issue individual or group accident and sickness insurance policies providing hospital, medical and surgical, or major medical coverage on an expense-incurred basis;

each health service corporation providing individual or group accident and sickness subscription contracts; and each health maintenance organization providing a health care plan for health care services shall provide coverage for the cost of such health care services provided through telehealth as directed through regulations promulgated by the Department.

(d) An insurer, health service corporation, or health maintenance organization shall not exclude a service for coverage solely because the service is provided through telemedicine services and is not provided through in-person consultation or contact between a health care provider and a patient for services appropriately provided through telemedicine services.

(e) An insurer, health service corporation, or health maintenance organization shall reimburse the treating provider or the consulting provider for the diagnosis, consultation or treatment of the insured delivered through telemedicine services on the same basis and at least at the rate that the insurer, health service corporation, or health maintenance organization is responsible for coverage for the provision of the same service through in-person consultation or contact. Payment for telemedicine interactions shall include reasonable compensation to the originating or distant site for the transmission cost incurred during the delivery of health care services.

(f) No insurer, health service corporation, or health maintenance organization shall impose any annual or lifetime dollar maximum on coverage for telemedicine services other than an annual or lifetime dollar maximum that applies in the aggregate to all items and services covered under the policy, or impose upon any person receiving benefits pursuant to this section any copayment, coinsurance, or deductible amounts, or any policy year, calendar year, lifetime, or other durational benefit limitation or maximum for benefits or services, that is not equally imposed upon all terms and services covered under the policy, contract or plan.

(g) The requirements of this section shall apply to all insurance policies, contracts, and plans delivered, issued for delivery, reissued, or extended on and after January 1, 2016, or at any time thereafter when any term of the policy, contract or plan is changed or any premium adjustment is made.

(h) This section shall not apply to short-term travel, accident-only, limited or specified disease, or individual conversion policies or contracts, nor shall it contravene any telehealth requirements made in policies or contracts designed for issuance to persons eligible for coverage under Titles XVIII, XIX, and XXI of the Social Security Act [42 U.S.C. §§ 1395 *et seq.*, 1396 *et seq.*, and 1397aa *et seq.*], known as Medicare, Medicaid, or any other similar coverage under state or federal governmental plans.

DISTRICT OF COLUMBIA

DC Code § 31-3861

Definitions

For the purposes of this chapter, the term:

(1) "Health benefits plan" shall have the same meaning as provided in § 31-3131(4).

(2) "Health insurer" shall have the same meaning as provided in § 31-3131(5).

(3) "Provider" shall have the same meaning as provided in § 31-3131(7).

(4) "Telehealth" means the delivery of healthcare services through the use of interactive audio, video or other electronic media used for the purpose of diagnosis, consultation or treatment; provided, that services delivered through audio-only telephones, electronic mail messages or facsimile transmissions are not included.

DC Code § 31-3862

Private reimbursement

(a) A health insurer offering a health benefits plan in the District may not deny coverage for a healthcare service on the basis that the service is provided through telehealth if the same service would be covered when delivered in person.

(b) A health insurer shall reimburse the provider for the diagnosis, consultation, or treatment of the insured when the service is delivered through telehealth.

(c) A health insurer shall not be required to:

(1) Reimburse a provider for health care service delivered through telehealth that is not a covered under the health benefits plan; and

(2) Reimburse a provider who is not a covered provider under the health benefits plan.

(d) A health insurer may require a deductible, copayment or coinsurance amount for a health care service delivered through telehealth; provided, that the deductible, copayment or coinsurance amount may not exceed the amount applicable to the same service when it is delivered in person.

(e) A health insurer shall not impose any annual or lifetime dollar maximum on coverage for telehealth services other than an annual or lifetime dollar maximum that applies in the aggregate to all items and services under the health benefits plan.

(f) Nothing in this chapter shall preclude the health insurer from undertaking utilization review to determine the appropriateness of telehealth as a means of delivering a health care service; provided, that the determinations shall be made in the same manner as those regarding the same service when it is delivered in person.

FLORIDA
(NONE)

GEORGIA

GA Code 33-24-56.4

Payment for telemedicine services

(a) This Code section shall be known and may be cited as the "Georgia Telemedicine Act."

(b) As used in this Code section, the term:

(1) "Health benefit policy" means any individual or group plan, policy, or contract for health care services issued, delivered, issued for delivery, executed, or renewed in this state, including, but not limited to, those contracts executed by the State of Georgia on behalf of state employees under Article 1 of Chapter 18 of Title 45, by an insurer.

(2) "Insurer" means an accident and sickness insurer, fraternal benefit society, hospital service corporation, medical service corporation, health care corporation, health maintenance organization, preferred provider organization, provider sponsored health care corporation, managed care entity, or any similar entity authorized to issue contracts under this title or to provide health benefit policies.

(3) "Telemedicine" means the practice, by a duly licensed physician or other health care provider acting within the scope of such provider's practice, of health care delivery, diagnosis, consultation, treatment, or transfer of medical data by means of audio, video, or data communications which are used during a medical visit with a patient or which are used to transfer medical data obtained during a medical visit with a patient. Standard telephone, facsimile transmissions, unsecured e-mail, or a combination thereof do not constitute telemedicine services.

(c) It is the intent of the General Assembly to mitigate geographic discrimination in the delivery of health care by recognizing the application of and payment for covered medical care provided by means of telemedicine, provided that such services are provided by a physician or by another health care practitioner or professional acting within the scope of practice of such health care practitioner or professional and in accordance with the provisions of Code Section 43-34-31.

(d) On and after July 1, 2005, every health benefit policy that is issued, amended, or renewed shall include payment for services that are covered under such health benefit policy and are appropriately provided through telemedicine in accordance with Code Section 43-34-31 and generally accepted health care practices and standards prevailing in the applicable professional community at the time the services were provided. The coverage required in this Code section may be subject to all terms and conditions of the applicable health benefit plan.

HAWAII

HI Statutes §§ 431:10A 116.3

Coverage for telehealth

(a) It is the intent of the legislature to recognize the application of telehealth as a reimbursable service by which an individual shall receive medical services from a health care provider without face-to-face contact with the health care provider.

(b) No accident and health or sickness insurance plan that is issued, amended or renewed shall require face-to-face contact between a health care provider and a patient as a prerequisite for payment for services appropriately provided through telehealth in accordance with generally accepted health care practices and standards prevailing in the applicable professional community at the time the services were provided. The coverage required in this section may be subject to all terms and conditions of the plan agreed upon among the enrollee or subscriber, the insurer, and the health care provider.

(c) Reimbursement for services provided through telehealth shall be equivalent to reimbursement for the same services provided via face-to-face contact between a health care provider and a patient. Nothing in this section shall require a health care provider to be physically present with the patient at an originating site unless a health care provider at the distant site deems it necessary.

(d) Notwithstanding chapter 453 or rules adopted pursuant thereto, in the event that a health care provider-patient relationship does not exist between the patient and the health care provider to be involved in a telehealth interaction between the patient and the health care provider, a telehealth mechanism may be used to establish a health care provider-patient relationship.

(e) All insurers shall provide current and prospective insureds with written disclosure of coverages and benefits associated with telehealth services, including information on copayments, deductibles or coinsurance requirements under a policy, contract, plan or agreement. The information provided shall be current, understandable, and available prior to the issuance of a policy, contract, plan or agreement, and upon request after the policy, contract, plan or agreement has been issued.

(f) Services provided by telehealth pursuant to this section shall be consistent with all federal and state privacy, security and confidentiality laws.

(g) For the purposes of this section:

"Distant site" means the location of the health care provider delivering services through telehealth at the time the services are provided.

"Health care provider" means a provider of services, as defined in title 42 United States Code section 1395x(u), a provider of medical and other health services, as defined in title 42 United States Code section 1395x(s), other practitioners licensed by the State and working within their scope of practice, and any other person or organization who furnishes, bills, or is paid for health care in the normal course of business, including but not limited to primary care providers, mental health providers, oral health providers, physicians and osteopathic physicians licensed under chapter 453, advanced practice registered nurses licensed under chapter 457, psychologists licensed under chapter 465, and dentists licensed under chapter 448.

"Originating site" means the location where the patient is located, whether accompanied or not by a health care provider, at the time services are provided by a health care provider through telehealth, including but not limited to a health care provider's office, hospital, health care facility, a patient's home, and other nonmedical environments such as school-based health centers, university-based health centers, or the work location of a patient.

"Telehealth" means the use of telecommunications services, as defined in section 269-1, to encompass four modalities: store and forward technologies, remote monitoring, live consultation, and mobile health; and which shall include but not be limited to real-time video conferencing-based communication, secure interactive and non-interactive web-based communication, and secure asynchronous information exchange, to transmit patient medical information, including diagnostic-quality digital images and laboratory results for medical interpretation and diagnosis, for the purpose of delivering enhanced health care services and information while a patient is at an originating site and the health care provider is at a distant site. Standard telephone contacts, facsimile transmissions or e-mail text, in combination or by itself, does not constitute a telehealth service for the purposes of this chapter.

IDAHO

(NONE)

ILLINOIS

(NONE)

IOWA

(NONE)

KANSAS

(NONE)

KENTUCKY

KRS § 304.17A-138

Prohibition against health benefit plan excluding coverage for telehealth; benefits subject to deductible, copayment, or coinsurance; payment subject to provider network arrangements; administrative regulations

(1) (a) A health benefit plan shall not exclude a service from coverage solely because the service is provided through telehealth and not provided through a face-to-face consultation if the consultation is provided through the telehealth network established under KRS 194A.125. A health benefit plan may provide coverage for a consultation at a site not within the telehealth network at the discretion of the insurer.

(b) A telehealth consultation shall not be reimbursable under this section if it is provided through the use of an audio-only telephone, facsimile machine or electronic mail.

(2) Benefits for a service provided through telehealth required by this section may be made subject to a deductible, copayment or coinsurance requirement. A deductible, copayment or coinsurance applicable to a particular service provided through telehealth shall not exceed the deductible, copayment or coinsurance required by the health benefit plan for the same service provided through a face-to-face consultation.

(3) Payment made under this section may be consistent with any provider network arrangements that have been established for the health benefit plan.

(4) The department shall promulgate an administrative regulation in accordance with KRS Chapter 13A to designate the claim forms and records required to be maintained in conjunction with this section.

907 KAR 3:170

Telehealth consultation coverage and reimbursement.

Section 5. Reimbursement. (1) (a) The department shall reimburse a telehealth provider who is eligible for reimbursement from the department for a telehealth consultation an amount equal to the amount paid for a comparable in-person service in accordance with:

1. 907 KAR 3:010 if the service was provided:

a. By a physician; and

b. Not in the circumstances described in subparagraphs 3., 4., 5., or 6. of this paragraph;

2. 907 KAR 1:104 if the service was provided:

a. By an advanced practice registered nurse; and

b. Not in the circumstances described in subparagraphs 3., 4., 5., or 6. of this paragraph;

3. 907 KAR 1:055 if the service was provided and billed through a federally-qualified health center, federally-qualified health center look-alike, rural health clinic or primary care center;

4. 907 KAR 1:015 if the service was provided and billed through a hospital outpatient department;

5. 907 KAR 1:031 if the service was provided and billed through a home health agency; or

6. 907 KAR 1:065 if the service was provided and billed through a nursing facility.

(b) 1. Reimbursement for a telehealth consultation provided by a practitioner who is employed by a provider or is an agent of a provider shall be a matter between the provider and the practitioner.

2. The department shall not be liable for reimbursing a practitioner who is employed by a provider or is an agent of a provider.

(c) A managed care organization shall not be required to reimburse the same amount for a telehealth consultation as the department reimburses, but may reimburse the same amount as the department reimburses if the managed care organization chooses to do so.

(2) A telehealth provider shall bill for a telehealth consultation using the appropriate two (2) letter "GT" modifier.

(3) The department shall not require the presence of a health care provider requesting a telehealth consultation at the time of the telehealth consultation unless it is requested by a telehealth provider or telehealth practitioner at the hub site.

(4) The department shall not reimburse for transmission costs.

LOUISIANA

LSA-RS 22:1821

§ 1821. Payment of claims; health and accident policies; prospective review; penalties; self insurers; telemedicine reimbursement by insurers

A. All claims arising under the terms of health and accident contracts issued in this state, except as provided in Subsection B of this Section, shall be paid not more than thirty days from the date upon which written notice and proof of claim, in the form required by the terms of the policy, are furnished to the insurer unless just and reasonable grounds, such as would put a reasonable and prudent businessman on his guard, exist. The insurer shall make payment at least every thirty days to the assured during that part of the period of his disability covered by the policy or contract of insurance during which the insured is entitled to such payments. Failure to comply with the provisions of this Section shall subject the insurer to a penalty payable to the insured of double the amount of the health and accident benefits due under the terms of the policy or contract during the period of delay, together with attorney fees to be determined by the court. Any court of competent jurisdiction in the parish where the insured lives or has his domicile, excepting a justice of the peace court, shall have jurisdiction to try such cases.

B. All claims for accidental death arising under the terms of health and accident contracts where such contracts insure against accidental death shall be settled by the insurer within sixty days of receipt of due proof of death and should the insurer fail to do so without just cause, then the amount due shall bear interest at the rate of six percent per annum from date of receipt of due proof of death by the insurer until paid.

C. Any person, partnership, corporation or other organization, or the State of Louisiana which provides or contracts to provide health and accident benefit coverage as a self-insurer for his or its employees, stockholders or any other persons, shall be subject to the provisions of this Section, including the provisions relating to penalties and attorney fees, without regard to whether the person or organization is a commercial insurer; however, this Section shall not apply to collectively bargained union welfare plans other than health and accident plans.

D. (1) In any event where the contract between an insurer or self-insurer and the insured is issued or delivered in this state and contains a provision that in non-emergency cases the insured is required to be prospectively evaluated through a pre-hospital admission certification, pre-inpatient service eligibility program, or any similar pre-utilization review or screening procedure prior to the delivery of contemplated hospitalization, inpatient or outpatient health care, or medical services which are prescribed or ordered by a duly licensed health care provider who possesses admitting and clinical staff privileges at an acute care health care facility or ambulatory surgical care facility, the insurer, self-insurer, third-party administrator, or independent contractor shall be held liable in damages to the insured only for damages incurred or resulting from unreasonable delay, reduction, or denial of the proposed medically necessary services or care according to the information received from the health care provider at the time of the request for a prospective evaluation or review by the duly licensed health care provider, as provided in the contract; such damages shall be limited solely to the physical injuries which are the direct and proximate cause of the unreasonable delay, reduction, or denial as further defined in this Subsection together with reasonable attorney fees and court costs.

(2) (a) Any insurer, health maintenance organization, preferred provider organization or other managed care organization requirement that the insured be prospectively evaluated through a pre-hospital admission certification, pre-inpatient service eligibility program, or any similar pre-utilization review or screening procedure shall be inapplicable to an emergency medical condition.

(b) Every insurer, health maintenance organization, preferred provider organization or other managed care organization which includes emergency medical services as part of its policy or contract, shall provide coverage and shall subsequently pay providers for emergency medical services provided to an insured, enrollee, or patient who presents himself with an emergency medical condition. This Subparagraph shall not be construed to require coverage for illnesses, conditions, diseases, equipment, supplies or procedures or treatments which are not otherwise covered under the terms of the insured's policy or contract. The provisions of this Subparagraph shall not apply to hospital indemnity, disability, or renewable limited benefit supplemental health insurance policies authorized to be issued in this state.

(c) An insurer, health maintenance organization, preferred provider organization, or other managed care organization shall not retrospectively deny or reduce payments to providers for emergency medical services of an insured, enrollee, or patient even if it is determined that the emergency medical condition, initially presented is later identified through screening not to be an actual emergency, except in the following cases:

(i) Material misrepresentation, fraud, omission or clerical error.

(ii) Any payment reductions due to applicable copayments, coinsurance or deductibles which may be the responsibility of the insured.

(iii) Cases in which the insured does not meet the emergency medical condition definition, unless the insured has been referred to the emergency department by the insured's primary care physician or other agent acting on behalf of the insurer.

(d) Every insurer, health maintenance organization, preferred provider organization or other managed care organization shall inform its insureds, enrollees, patients and affiliated providers about all applicable policies related to emergency care access, coverage, payment and grievance procedures. It is the ultimate responsibility of the insurer, health maintenance organization or preferred provider organization to inform any contracted third party administrator, independent contractor or primary care provider about the emergency care provisions contained in this Paragraph.

(e) Failure to comply with the provisions of Subparagraphs (a), (b), and (c) of this Paragraph shall subject the insurer, health maintenance organization, preferred provider organization or other managed care organization to penalties as provided for in Subsection A of this Section and to penalties for violations as provided in R.S. 22:1969.

(f) The provisions of this Paragraph shall not apply to medical benefit plans that are established under and regulated by the Employment Retirement Income Security Act of 1974.

(g) As used in this Paragraph, the following definitions shall apply:

(i) "Emergency medical condition" is a medical condition of recent onset and severity, including severe pain, that would lead a prudent layperson, acting reasonably and possessing an average knowledge of health and medicine, to believe that the absence of immediate medical attention could reasonably be expected to result in:

(aa) Placing the health of the individual, or, with respect to a pregnant woman, the health of the woman or her unborn child, in serious jeopardy.

(bb) Serious impairment to bodily function.

(cc) Serious dysfunction of any bodily organ or part.

(ii) "Emergency medical services" are those medical services necessary to screen, evaluate and stabilize an emergency medical condition.

(iii) "Managed care organization" means a licensed insurance company, hospital or medical benefit plan or program, health maintenance organization, integrated health care delivery system, an employer or employee organization or a managed care contractor which operates a managed care plan. A managed care organization may include, but is not limited to, a preferred provider organization, health maintenance organization, exclusive provider organization, independent practice association, clinic without walls, management services organization, managed care services organization, physician hospital organization and hospital physician organization.

(iv) "Managed care plan" means a plan operated by a managed care entity which provides for the financing and delivery of health care and treatment services to individuals enrolled in such plan through its own employed health care providers or contracting with selected specific providers that conform to explicit selection, standards, or both. A managed care plan also customarily has a formal organizational structure for continual quality assurance, a certified utilization review program, dispute resolution, and financial incentives for individual enrollees to use the plan's participating providers and procedures.

(3) (a) For the purposes of this Subsection, a period of two working days from the time of the

duly licensed health care provider's request to the insurer, self-insurer, third party administrator or independent contractor for a pre-hospital admission or pre-inpatient service eligibility certification or any similar pre-utilization review or screening procedure confirmation until the receipt by the duly licensed health care provider of such insurer's, self-insurer's, third party administrator's or independent contractor's certification, approval or denial of the contemplated hospitalization, inpatient or outpatient health care, or medical services, shall not be considered unreasonable.

(b) For the purposes of this Subsection, a period in excess of two working days from the time of the duly licensed health care provider's request to the insurer, self-insurer, third party administrator or independent contractor for a pre-hospital admission or pre-inpatient service eligibility certification or any similar pre-utilization review or screening procedure confirmation until the receipt by the duly licensed health care provider of such insurer's, self-insurer's, third party administrator's, or independent contractor's certification, approval, or denial of the contemplated hospitalization, inpatient or outpatient health care, or medical services may be considered unreasonable depending on the circumstances of each individual case.

(c) For the purposes of this Subsection, the term "unreasonable reduction" shall mean the decreasing or limiting of either of the following:

(i) Previously certified or approved health care or medical services as contracted for between the insurer and insured.

(ii) Continued hospitalization and medical services without providing a procedure or method for certifying an extension of hospitalization and medical services by the insurer's or self-insurer's review or screening procedure in the event of continued hospitalization or medical attention, or both, as deemed medically necessary according to current established medical criteria.

(d) For the purposes of this Subsection, an "unreasonable denial" shall mean the failure to do any of the following:

(i) Review a request from a duly licensed health care provider by the insurer's or self-insurer's review or screening procedure.

(ii) Review a request from the insured within the time period as provided for in the contract between the insurer or self-insurer and the insured, which time period shall not exceed two work days as provided for in Subparagraph (a) of this Paragraph.

(iii) Deliver the contracted for health care or medical services previously certified or approved by the insurer's or self-insurer's review or screening procedure for medically necessary treatment or care as mandated by and provided for in the contract between the insurer or self-insurer and the insured.

(iv) Review a request from a duly licensed health care provider by the insurer's or self-insurer's review or screening procedure for an extension of the original certified or approved duration of health care or medical services.

(v) Extend the original certified or approved duration of hospitalization, health care or medical services requested by a duly licensed health care provider by the insurer's or self-insurer's review or screening procedure when treatment or care is deemed medically necessary according to current established medical criteria.

(e) For the purposes of this Subsection, "medically necessary treatment or care" shall mean contemplated hospitalization, inpatient or outpatient health care, or medical services recommended for appropriate treatment or care in accordance with nationally accepted current medical criteria.

(4) Any court of competent jurisdiction in the parish where the insured lives or has his domicile, excepting a justice of the peace court, has jurisdiction of cases arising under the provisions of Paragraph (1) of this Subsection.

E. No action for the recovery of penalties or attorney fees provided in this Section shall be brought after the expiration of one year after the date proofs of loss are required to be filed.

F. (1) Notwithstanding any provision of any policy or contract of insurance or health benefits issued, whenever such policy provides for payment, benefit or reimbursement for any health care service, including but not limited to diagnostic testing, treatment, referral or consultation, and such health care service is performed via transmitted electronic imaging or telemedicine, such a payment, benefit or reimbursement under such policy or contract shall not be denied to a licensed physician conducting or participating in the transmission at the originating health care facility or terminus who is physically present with the individual who is the subject of such electronic imaging transmission and is contemporaneously communicating and interacting with a licensed physician at the receiving terminus of the transmission. The payment, benefit or reimbursement to such a licensed physician at the originating facility or terminus shall not be less than seventy-five percent of the reasonable and customary amount of payment, benefit or reimbursement which that licensed physician receives for an intermediate office visit.

(2) Any health care service proposed to be performed or performed via transmitted electronic imaging or telemedicine under this Subsection shall be subject to the applicable utilization review criteria and requirements of the insurer. Terminology in a health and accident insurance policy or contract that either discriminates against or prohibits such a method of transmitted electronic imaging or telemedicine shall be void as against public policy of providing the highest quality health care to the citizens of the state.

(3) The provisions of this Subsection shall not apply to limited benefit health insurance policies or contracts authorized to be issued in the state.

MAINE

24-A MRSA § 4316

Coverage for telemedicine services

1. Definition. For the purposes of this section, "telemedicine," as it pertains to the delivery of health care services, means the use of interactive audio, video or other electronic media for the purpose of diagnosis, consultation or treatment. "Telemedicine" does not include the use of audio-only telephone, facsimile machine or e-mail.

2. Coverage of telemedicine services. A carrier offering a health plan in this State may not deny coverage on the basis that the coverage is provided through telemedicine if the health care service would be covered were it provided through in-person consultation between the covered person and a health care provider. Coverage for health care services provided through telemedicine must be determined in a manner consistent with coverage for health care services provided through in-person consultation. A carrier may offer a health plan containing a provision for a deductible, copayment or coinsurance requirement for a health care service provided through telemedicine as long as the deductible, copayment or coinsurance does not exceed the deductible, copayment or coinsurance applicable to an in-person consultation.

MARYLAND

MD Code, Insurance, § 15-139

Health care services delivered through telemedicine

Telemedicine defined

(a) (1) In this section, "telemedicine" means, as it relates to the delivery of health care services, the use of interactive audio, video, or other telecommunications or electronic technology by a licensed health care provider to deliver a health care service within the scope of practice of the health care provider at a site other than the site at which the patient is located.

(2) "Telemedicine" does not include:

(i) an audio-only telephone conversation between a health care provider and a patient;

(ii) an electronic mail message between a health care provider and a patient; or

(iii) a facsimile transmission between a health care provider and a patient.

Application of section

(b) This section applies to:

(1) insurers and nonprofit health service plans that provide hospital, medical or surgical benefits to individuals or groups on an expense-incurred basis under health insurance policies or contracts that are issued or delivered in the State; and

(2) health maintenance organizations that provide hospital, medical or surgical benefits to individuals or groups under contracts that are issued or delivered in the State.

Coverage for health care services delivered through telemedicine

(c) An entity subject to this section:

(1) shall provide coverage under a health insurance policy or contract for health care services appropriately delivered through telemedicine; and

(2) may not exclude from coverage a health care service solely because it is provided through telemedicine and is not provided through an in-person consultation or contact between a health care provider and a patient.

Reimbursement to health care provider for services delivered through telemedicine

(d) An entity subject to this section:

(1) shall reimburse a health care provider for the diagnosis, consultation and treatment of an insured patient for a health care service covered under a health insurance policy or contract that can be appropriately provided through telemedicine;

(2) is not required to:

(i) reimburse a health care provider for a health care service delivered in person or through telemedicine that is not a covered benefit under the health insurance policy or contract; or

(ii) reimburse a health care provider who is not a covered provider under the health insurance policy or contract; and

(3) (i) may impose a deductible, copayment or coinsurance amount on benefits for health care services that are delivered either through an in- person consultation or through telemedicine;

(ii) may impose an annual dollar maximum as permitted by federal law; and

(iii) may not impose a lifetime dollar maximum.

Utilization review to determine appropriateness of health care service

(e) An entity subject to this section may undertake utilization review, including preauthorization, to determine the appropriateness of any health care service whether the service is delivered through an in-person consultation or through telemedicine if the appropriateness of the health care service is determined in the same manner.

Policies or contracts not to distinguish between patients in rural or urban locations

(f) A health insurance policy or contract may not distinguish between patients in rural or urban locations in providing coverage under the policy or contract for health care services delivered through telemedicine.

Decision by entity not to provide coverage for telemedicine

(g) A decision by an entity subject to this section not to provide coverage for telemedicine in accordance with this section constitutes an adverse decision, as defined in § 15-10A-01 of this title, if the decision is based on a finding that telemedicine is not medically necessary, appropriate, or efficient.

MASSACHUSETTS

MGLA 175 § 47BB

Coverage for telemedicine services

(a) For the purposes of this section, "telemedicine" as it pertains to the delivery of health care services, shall mean the use of interactive audio, video or other electronic media for the purpose of diagnosis, consultation or treatment. "Telemedicine" shall not include the use of audio-only telephone, facsimile machine or e-mail.

(b) An insurer may limit coverage of telemedicine services to those health care providers in a telemedicine network approved by the insurer.

(c) A contract that provides coverage for services under this section may contain a provision for a deductible, copayment or coinsurance requirement for a health care service provided through telemedicine as long as the deductible, copayment or coinsurance does not exceed the deductible, copayment or coinsurance applicable to an in-person consultation,

(d) Coverage for health care services under this section shall be consistent with coverage for health care services provided through in-person consultation.

MICHIGAN

MCLA 550.1401k

Telemedicine services

Sec. 401k. (1) A group or non-group health care corporation certificate shall not require face-to-face contact between a health care professional and a patient for services appropriately provided through telemedicine, as determined by the health care corporation. Telemedicine services shall be provided by a health care professional who is licensed, registered, or otherwise authorized to engage in his or her health care profession in the state where the patient is located. Telemedicine services are subject to all terms and conditions of the certificate agreed upon between the certificate holder and the health care corporation, including, but not limited to, required copayments, coinsurances, deductibles and approved amounts.

(2) As used in this section, "telemedicine" means the use of an electronic media to link patients with health care professionals in different locations. To be considered telemedicine under this section, the health care professional must be able to examine the patient via a real-time, interactive audio or video, or both, telecommunications system and the patient must be able to interact with the off-site health care professional at the time the services are provided.

(3) This section applies to a certificate issued or renewed on or after January 1, 2013.

MCLA 500.3476

Coverage for telemedicine services

Sec. 3476. (1) An insurer that delivers, issues for delivery, or renews in this state a health insurance policy shall not require face-to-face contact between a health care professional and a patient for services appropriately provided through telemedicine, as determined by the insurer. Telemedicine services must be provided by a health care professional who is licensed, registered, or otherwise authorized to engage in his or her health care profession in the state where the patient is located. Telemedicine services are subject to all terms and conditions of the health insurance policy agreed upon between the policy holder and the insurer, including, but not limited to, required copayments, coinsurances, deductibles and approved amounts.

(2) As used in this section, "telemedicine" means the use of an electronic media to link patients with health care professionals in different locations. To be considered telemedicine under this section, the health care professional must be able to examine the patient via a real-time, interactive audio or video, or both, telecommunications system and the patient must be able to interact with the off-site health care professional at the time the services are provided.

MINNESOTA

MSA § 62A.672

Coverage of telemedicine services

Subdivision 1. Coverage of telemedicine.

(a) A health plan sold, issued, or renewed by a health carrier for which coverage of benefits begins on or after January 1, 2017, shall include coverage for telemedicine benefits in the same manner as any other benefits covered under the policy, plan or contract, and shall comply with the regulations of this section.

(b) Nothing in this section shall be construed to:

(1) require a health carrier to provide coverage for services that are not medically necessary;

(2) prohibit a health carrier from establishing criteria that a health care provider must meet to demonstrate the safety or efficacy of delivering a particular service via telemedicine for which the health carrier does not already reimburse other health care providers for delivering via telemedicine, so long as the criteria are not unduly burdensome or unreasonable for the particular service; or

(3) prevent a health carrier from requiring a health care provider to agree to certain documentation or billing practices designed to protect the health carrier or patients from fraudulent claims so long as the practices are not unduly burdensome or unreasonable for the particular service.

Subd. 2. Parity between telemedicine and in-person services.

A health carrier shall not exclude a service for coverage solely because the service is provided via telemedicine and is not provided through in-person consultation or contact between a licensed health care provider and a patient.

Subd. 3. Reimbursement for telemedicine services.

(a) A health carrier shall reimburse the distant site licensed health care provider for covered services delivered via telemedicine on the same basis and at the same rate as the health carrier would apply to those services if the services had been delivered in person by the distant site licensed health care provider.

(b) It is not a violation of this subdivision for a health carrier to include a deductible, copayment or coinsurance requirement for a health care service provided via telemedicine, provided that the deductible, copayment or coinsurance is not in addition to, and does not exceed, the deductible, copayment or coinsurance applicable if the same services were provided through in-person contact.

MISSISSIPPI

Miss. Code Ann. § 83-9-351

Telemedicine services coverage

(1) As used in this section:

(a) "Employee benefit plan" means any plan, fund or program established or maintained by an employer or by an employee organization, or both, to the extent that such plan, fund or program was established or is maintained for the purpose of providing for its participants or their beneficiaries, through the purchase of insurance or otherwise, medical, surgical, hospital care or other benefits.

(b) "Health insurance plan" means any health insurance policy or health benefit plan offered by a health insurer, and includes the State and School Employees Health Insurance Plan and any other public health care assistance program offered or administered by the state or any political subdivision or instrumentality of the state. The term does not include policies or plans providing coverage for specified disease or other limited benefit coverage.

(c) "Health insurer" means any health insurance company, nonprofit hospital and medical service corporation, health maintenance organization, preferred provider organization, managed care organization, pharmacy benefit manager, and, to the extent permitted under federal law, any administrator of an insured, self-insured or publicly funded health care benefit plan offered by public and private entities, and other parties that are by statute, contract, or agreement, legally responsible for payment of a claim for a health care item or service.

(d) "Telemedicine" means the delivery of health care services such as diagnosis, consultation or treatment through the use of interactive audio, video or other electronic media. Telemedicine must be "real-time" consultation, and it does not include the use of audio-only telephone, e-mail or facsimile.

(2) All health insurance and employee benefit plans in this state must provide coverage for telemedicine services to the same extent that the services would be covered if they were provided through in-person consultation.

(3) A health insurance or employee benefit plan may charge a deductible, copayment or coinsurance for a health care service provided through telemedicine so long as it does not exceed the deductible, copayment or coinsurance applicable to an in-person consultation.

(4) A health insurance or employee benefit plan may limit coverage to health care providers in a telemedicine network approved by the plan.

(5) Nothing in this section shall be construed to prohibit a health insurance or employee benefit plan from providing coverage for only those services that are medically necessary, subject to the terms and conditions of the covered person's policy.

(6) In a claim for the services provided, the appropriate procedure code for the covered services shall be included with the appropriate modifier indicating interactive communication was used.

(7) The originating site is eligible to receive a facility fee, but facility fees are not payable to the distant site.

Miss. Code Ann. § 83-9-353

Requirement to provide coverage and reimburse for telemedicine and remote patient monitoring services

(1) As used in this section:

(a) "Employee benefit plan" means any plan, fund or program established or maintained by an employer or by an employee organization, or both, to the extent that such plan, fund or program was established or is maintained for the purpose of providing for its participants or their beneficiaries, through the purchase of insurance or otherwise, medical, surgical, hospital care or other benefits.

(b) "Health insurance plan" means any health insurance policy or health benefit plan offered by a health insurer, and includes the State and School Employees Health Insurance Plan and any other public health care assistance program offered or administered by the state or any political subdivision or instrumentality of the state. The term does not include policies or plans providing coverage for specified disease or other limited benefit coverage.

(c) "Health insurer" means any health insurance company, nonprofit hospital and medical service corporation, health maintenance organization, preferred provider organization, managed care organization, pharmacy benefit manager, and, to the extent permitted under federal law, any administrator of an insured, self-insured or publicly funded health care benefit plan offered by public and private entities, and other parties that are by statute, contract, or agreement, legally responsible for payment of a claim for a health care item or service.

(d) "Store-and-forward telemedicine services" means the use of asynchronous computer based communication between a patient and a consulting provider or a referring health care provider and a medical specialist at a distant site for the purpose of diagnostic and therapeutic assistance in the care of patients who otherwise have no access to specialty care. Store-and-forward telemedicine services involve the transferring of medical data from one (1) site to another through the use of a camera or similar device that records (stores) an image that is sent (forwarded) via telecommunication to another site for consultation.

(e) "Remote patient monitoring services" means the delivery of home health services using telecommunications technology to enhance the delivery of home health care, including:

(i) Monitoring of clinical patient data such as weight, blood pressure, pulse, pulse oximetry and other condition-specific data, such as blood glucose;

(ii) Medication adherence monitoring; and

(iii) Interactive video conferencing with or without digital image upload as needed.

(f) "Mediation adherence management services" means the monitoring of a patient's conformance with the clinician's medication plan with respect to timing, dosing and frequency of medication-taking through electronic transmission of data in a home telemonitoring program.

(2) Store-and-forward telemedicine services allow a health care provider trained and licensed in his or her given specialty to review forwarded images and patient history in order to provide diagnostic and therapeutic assistance in the care of the patient without the patient being present in real time. Treatment recommendations made via electronic means shall be held to the same standards of appropriate practice as those in traditional provider-patient setting.

(3) Any patient receiving medical care by store-and-forward telemedicine services shall be notified of the right to receive interactive communication with the distant specialist health care provider and shall receive an interactive communication with the distant specialist upon request. If requested, communication with the distant specialist may occur at the time of the consultation or within thirty (30) days of the patient's notification of the request of the consultation. Telemedicine networks unable to offer the interactive consultation shall not be reimbursed for store-and-forward telemedicine services.

(4) Remote patient monitoring services aim to allow more people to remain at home or in other residential settings and to improve the quality and cost of their care, including prevention of more costly care. Remote patient monitoring services via telehealth aim to coordinate primary, acute, behavioral and long-term social service needs for high-need, high-cost patients. Specific patient criteria must be met in order for reimbursement to occur.

(5) Qualifying patients for remote patient monitoring services must meet all the following criteria:

(a) Be diagnosed, in the last eighteen (18) months, with one or more chronic conditions, as defined by the Centers for Medicare and Medicaid Services (CMS), which include, but are not limited to, sickle cell, mental health, asthma, diabetes and heart disease;

(b) Have a recent history of costly service use due to one or more chronic conditions as evidenced by two (2) or more hospitalizations, including emergency room visits, in the last twelve (12) months; and

(c) The patient's health care provider recommends disease management services via remote patient monitoring.

(6) A remote patient monitoring prior authorization request form must be submitted to request telemonitoring services. The request must include the following:

(a) An order for home telemonitoring services, signed and dated by the prescribing physician;

(b) A plan of care, signed and dated by the prescribing physician, that includes telemonitoring transmission frequency and duration of monitoring requested;

(c) The client's diagnosis and risk factors that qualify the client for home telemonitoring services;

(d) Attestation that the client is sufficiently cognitively intact and able to operate the equipment or has a willing and able person to assist in completing electronic transmission of data; and

(e) Attestation that the client is not receiving duplicative services via disease management services.

(7) The entity that will provide the remote monitoring must be a Mississippi-based entity and have protocols in place to address all of the following:

(a) Authentication and authorization of users;

(b) A mechanism for monitoring, tracking and responding to changes in a client's clinical condition;

(c) A standard of acceptable and unacceptable parameters for client's clinical parameters, which can be adjusted based on the client's condition;

(d) How monitoring staff will respond to abnormal parameters for client's vital signs, symptoms and/or lab results;

(e) The monitoring, tracking and responding to changes in client's clinical condition;

(f) The process for notifying the prescribing physician for significant changes in the client's clinical signs and symptoms;

(g) The prevention of unauthorized access to the system or information;

(h) System security, including the integrity of information that is collected, program integrity and system integrity;

(i) Information storage, maintenance and transmission;

(j) Synchronization and verification of patient profile data; and

(k) Notification of the client's discharge from remote patient monitoring services or the de-installation of the remote patient monitoring unit.

(8) The telemonitoring equipment must:

(a) Be capable of monitoring any data parameters in the plan of care; and

(b) Be a FDA Class II hospital-grade medical device.

(9) Monitoring of the client's data shall not be duplicated by another provider.

(10) To receive payment for the delivery of remote patient monitoring services via telehealth, the service must involve:

(a) An assessment, problem identification, and evaluation that includes:

(i) Assessment and monitoring of clinical data including, but not limited to, appropriate vital signs, pain levels and other biometric measures specified in the plan of care, and also includes assessment of response to previous changes in the plan of care; and

(ii) Detection of condition changes based on the telemedicine encounter that may indicate the need for a change in the plan of care.

(b) Implementation of a management plan through one or more of the following:

(i) Teaching regarding medication management as appropriate based on the telemedicine findings for that encounter;

(ii) Teaching regarding other interventions as appropriate to both the patient and the caregiver;

(iii) Management and evaluation of the plan of care including changes in visit frequency or addition of other skilled services;

(iv) Coordination of care with the ordering health care provider regarding telemedicine findings;

(v) Coordination and referral to other medical providers as needed; and

(vi) Referral for an in-person visit or the emergency room as needed.

(11) The telemedicine equipment and network used for remote patient monitoring services should meet the following requirements:

(a) Comply with applicable standards of the United States Food and Drug Administration;

(b) Telehealth equipment be maintained in good repair and free from safety hazards;

(c) Telehealth equipment be new or sanitized before installation in the patient's home setting;

(d) Accommodate non-English language options; and

(e) Have 24/7 technical and clinical support services available for the patient user.

(12) All health insurance and employee benefit plans in this state must provide coverage and reimbursement for the asynchronous telemedicine services of store-and-forward telemedicine services and remote patient monitoring services based on the criteria set out in this section. Store-and-forward telemedicine services shall be reimbursed to the same extent that the services would be covered if they were provided through in-person consultation.

(13) Remote patient monitoring services shall include reimbursement for a daily monitoring rate at a minimum of Ten Dollars ($10.00) per day each month and Sixteen Dollars ($16.00) per day when medication adherence management services are included, not to exceed thirty-one (31) days per month. These reimbursement rates are only eligible to Mississippi-based telehealth programs affiliated with a Mississippi health care facility.

(14) A one-time telehealth installation/training fee for remote patient monitoring services will also be reimbursed at a minimum rate of Fifty Dollars ($50.00) per patient, with a maximum of two (2) installation/training fees/calendar year. These reimbursement rates are only eligible to Mississippi-based telehealth programs affiliated with a Mississippi health care facility.

(15) No geographic restrictions shall be placed on the delivery of telemedicine services in the home setting other than requiring the patient reside within the State of Mississippi.

(16) Health care providers seeking reimbursement for store-and-forward telemedicine services must be licensed Mississippi providers that are affiliated with an established Mississippi health care facility in order to qualify for reimbursement of telemedicine services in the state. If a service is not available in Mississippi, then a health insurance or employee benefit plan may decide to allow a non-Mississippi-based provider who is licensed to practice in Mississippi reimbursement for those services.

(17) A health insurance or employee benefit plan may charge a deductible, copayment or coinsurance for a health care service provided through store-and-forward telemedicine services or remote patient monitoring services so long as it does not exceed the deductible, copayment or coinsurance applicable to an in-person consultation.

(18) A health insurance or employee benefit plan may limit coverage to health care providers in a telemedicine network approved by the plan.

(19) Nothing in this section shall be construed to prohibit a health insurance or employee benefit plan from providing coverage for only those services that are medically necessary, subject to the terms and conditions of the covered person's policy.

(20) In a claim for the services provided, the appropriate procedure code for the covered service shall be included with the appropriate modifier indicating telemedicine services were used. A "GQ" modifier is required for asynchronous telemedicine services such as store-and-forward and remote patient monitoring.

(21) The originating site is eligible to receive a facility fee, but facility fees are not payable to the distant site.

MISSOURI

VAMS 376.1900

Definitions—coverage for health care services provided through telehealth—reimbursement, copayments, coinsurance, deductible amount, utilization reviews, supplemental insurance policies

1. As used in this section, the following terms shall mean:

(1) "Electronic visit," or "e-visit," an online electronic medical evaluation and management service completed using a secured web-based or similar electronic-based communications network for a single patient encounter. An electronic visit shall be initiated by a patient or by the guardian of a patient with the health care provider, be completed using a federal Health Insurance Portability and Accountability Act (HIPAA)-compliant online connection, and include a permanent record of the electronic visit;

(2) "Health benefit plan" shall have the same meaning ascribed to it in section 376.1350;

(3) "Health care provider" shall have the same meaning ascribed to it in section 376.1350;

(4) "Health care service", a service for the diagnosis, prevention, treatment, cure or relief of a physical or mental health condition, illness, injury or disease;

(5) "Health carrier" shall have the same meaning ascribed to it in section 376.1350;

(6) "Telehealth" shall have the same meaning ascribed to it in section 208.670.

2. Each health carrier or health benefit plan that offers or issues health benefit plans which are delivered, issued for delivery, continued, or renewed in this state on or after January 1, 2014, shall not deny coverage for a health care service on the basis that the health care service is provided through telehealth if the same service would be covered if provided through face-to-face diagnosis, consultation or treatment.

3. A health carrier may not exclude an otherwise covered health care service from coverage solely because the service is provided through telehealth rather than face-to-face consultation or contact between a health care provider and a patient.

4. A health carrier shall not be required to reimburse a telehealth provider or a consulting provider for site origination fees or costs for the provision of telehealth services; however, subject to correct coding, a health carrier shall reimburse a health care provider for the diagnosis, consultation or treatment of an insured or enrollee when the health care service is delivered through telehealth on the same basis that the health carrier covers the service when it is delivered in person.

5. A health care service provided through telehealth shall not be subject to any greater deductible, copayment or coinsurance amount than would be applicable if the same health care service was provided through face-to-face diagnosis, consultation or treatment.

6. A health carrier shall not impose upon any person receiving benefits under this section any

copayment, coinsurance, or deductible amount, or any policy year, calendar year, lifetime or other durational benefit limitation or maximum for benefits or services that is not equally imposed upon all terms and services covered under the policy, contract or health benefit plan.

7. Nothing in this section shall preclude a health carrier from undertaking utilization review to determine the appropriateness of telehealth as a means of delivering a health care service, provided that the determinations shall be made in the same manner as those regarding the same service when it is delivered in person.

8. A health carrier or health benefit plan may limit coverage for health care services that are provided through telehealth to health care providers that are in a network approved by the plan or the health carrier.

9. Nothing in this section shall be construed to require a health care provider to be physically present with a patient where the patient is located unless the health care provider who is providing health care services by means of telehealth determines that the presence of a health care provider is necessary.

10. The provisions of this section shall not apply to a supplemental insurance policy, including a life care contract, accident-only policy, specified disease policy, hospital policy providing a fixed daily benefit only, Medicare supplement policy, long-term care policy, short-term major medical policies of six months' or less duration, or any other supplemental policy as determined by the director of the department of insurance, financial institutions and professional registration.

MONTANA

MCA 33-22-138

Coverage for telemedicine services

(1) Each group or individual policy, certificate of disability insurance, subscriber contract, membership contract or health care services agreement that provides coverage for health care services must provide coverage for health care services provided by a health care provider or health care facility by means of telemedicine if the services are otherwise covered by the policy, certificate, contract or agreement.

(2) Coverage under this section must be equivalent to the coverage for services that are provided in person by a health care provider or health care facility.

(3) Nothing in this section may be construed to require:

(a) a health insurance issuer to provide coverage for services that are not medically necessary, subject to the terms and conditions of the insured's policy; or

(b) a health care provider to be physically present with a patient at the site where the patient is located unless the health care provider who is providing health care services by means of telemedicine determines that the presence of a health care provider is necessary.

(4) Coverage under this section may be subject to deductibles, coinsurance and copayment provisions. Special deductible, coinsurance, copayment or other limitations that are not generally applicable to other medical services covered under the plan may not be imposed on the coverage for services provided by means of telemedicine.

(5) This section does not apply to disability income, hospital indemnity, Medicare supplement, specified disease or long-term care policies.

(6) For the purposes of this section, the following definitions apply:

(a) "Health care facility" means a critical access hospital, hospice, hospital, long-term care facility, mental health center, outpatient center for primary care or outpatient center for surgical services licensed pursuant to Title 50, chapter 5.

(b) "Health care provider" means an individual:

(i) licensed pursuant to Title 37, chapter 3, 6, 7, 10, 11, 15, 17, 20, 22, 23, 24, 25 or 35;

(ii) licensed pursuant to Title 37, chapter 8, to practice as a registered professional nurse or as an advanced practice registered nurse;

(iii) certified by the American board of genetic counseling as a genetic counselor; or

(iv) certified by the national certification board for diabetes educators as a diabetes educator.

(c) "Store-and-forward technology" means electronic information, imaging and communication that is transferred, recorded or otherwise stored in order to be reviewed at a later date by a health care provider or health care facility at a distant site without the patient present in real time. The term includes interactive audio, video and data communication.

(d) (i) "Telemedicine" means the use of interactive audio, video or other telecommunications technology that is:

(A) used by a health care provider or health care facility to deliver health care services at a site other than the site where the patient is located; and

(B) delivered over a secure connection that complies with the requirements of the Health Insurance Portability and Accountability Act of 1996, 42 U.S.C. 1320d, *et seq.*

(ii) The term includes the use of electronic media for consultation relating to the health care diagnosis or treatment of a patient in real time or through the use of store-and-forward technology.

(iii) The term does not include the use of audio-only telephone, e-mail or facsimile transmissions.

NEBRASKA
(NONE)

NEVADA

NRS 689C.195

Coverage for services provided through telehealth

1. A health benefit plan must include coverage for services provided to an insured through telehealth to the same extent as though provided in person or by other means.

2. A carrier shall not:

(a) Require an insured to establish a relationship in person with a provider of health care or provide any additional consent to or reason for obtaining services through telehealth as a condition to providing the coverage described in subsection 1;

(b) Require a provider of health care to demonstrate that it is necessary to provide services to an insured through telehealth or receive any additional type of certification or license to provide services through telehealth as a condition to providing the coverage described in subsection 1;

(c) Refuse to provide the coverage described in subsection 1 because of the distant site from which a provider of health care provides services through telehealth or the originating site at which an insured receives services through telehealth; or

(d) Require covered services to be provided through telehealth as a condition to providing coverage for such services.

3. A health benefit plan must not require an insured to obtain prior authorization for any service provided through telehealth that is not required for the service when provided in person. A health benefit plan may require prior authorization for a service provided through telehealth if such prior authorization would be required if the service were provided in person or by other means.

4. The provisions of this section do not require a carrier to:

(a) Ensure that covered services are available to an insured through telehealth at a particular originating site;

(b) Provide coverage for a service that is not a covered service or that is not provided by a covered provider of health care; or

(c) Enter into a contract with any provider of health care or cover any service if the carrier is not otherwise required by law to do so.

5. A plan subject to the provisions of this chapter that is delivered, issued for delivery or renewed on or after July 1, 2015, has the legal effect of including the coverage required by this section, and any provision of the plan or the renewal which is in conflict with this section is void.

6. As used in this section:

(a) "Distant site" has the meaning ascribed to it in NRS 629.515.

(b) "Originating site" has the meaning ascribed to it in NRS 629.515.

(c) "Provider of health care" has the meaning ascribed to it in NRS 439.820.

(d) "Telehealth" has the meaning ascribed to it in NRS 629.515.

NRS 695A.265

Coverage for services provided through telehealth

1. A benefit contract must include coverage for services provided to an insured through telehealth to the same extent as though provided in person or by other means.

2. A society shall not:

(a) Require an insured to establish a relationship in person with a provider of health care or provide any additional consent to or reason for obtaining services through telehealth as a condition to providing the coverage described in subsection 1;

(b) Require a provider of health care to demonstrate that it is necessary to provide services to an insured through telehealth or receive any additional type of certification or license to provide services through telehealth as a condition to providing the coverage described in subsection 1;

(c) Refuse to provide the coverage described in subsection 1 because of the distant site from which a provider of health care provides services through telehealth or the originating site at which an insured receives services through telehealth; or

(d) Require covered services to be provided through telehealth as a condition to providing coverage for such services.

3. A benefit contract must not require an insured to obtain prior authorization for any service provided through telehealth that is not required for the service when provided in person. A benefit contract may require prior authorization for a service provided through telehealth if such prior authorization would be required if the service were provided in person or by other means.

4. The provisions of this section do not require a society to:

(a) Ensure that covered services are available to an insured through telehealth at a particular originating site;

(b) Provide coverage for a service that is not a covered service or that is not provided by a covered provider of health care; or

(c) Enter into a contract with any provider of health care or cover any service if the society is not otherwise required by law to do so.

5. A benefit contract subject to the provisions of this chapter that is delivered, issued for delivery or renewed on or after July 1, 2015, has the legal effect of including the coverage required by this

section, and any provision of the contract or the renewal which is in conflict with this section is void.

6. As used in this section:

(a) "Distant site" has the meaning ascribed to it in NRS 629.515.

(b) "Originating site" has the meaning ascribed to it in NRS 629.515.

(c) "Provider of health care" has the meaning ascribed to it in NRS 439.820.

(d) "Telehealth" has the meaning ascribed to it in NRS 629.515.

NRS 689A.0463

Coverage for services provided through telehealth; prohibited actions by insurer; exclusions

1. A policy of health insurance must include coverage for services provided to an insured through telehealth to the same extent as though provided in person or by other means.

2. An insurer shall not:

(a) Require an insured to establish a relationship in person with a provider of health care or provide any additional consent to or reason for obtaining services through telehealth as a condition to providing the coverage described in subsection 1;

(b) Require a provider of health care to demonstrate that it is necessary to provide services to an insured through telehealth or receive any additional type of certification or license to provide services through telehealth as a condition to providing the coverage described in subsection 1;

(c) Refuse to provide the coverage described in subsection 1 because of the distant site from which a provider of health care provides services through telehealth or the originating site at which an insured receives services through telehealth; or

(d) Require covered services to be provided through telehealth as a condition to providing coverage for such services.

3. A policy of health insurance must not require an insured to obtain prior authorization for any service provided through telehealth that is not required for the service when provided in person. A policy of health insurance may require prior authorization for a service provided through telehealth if such prior authorization would be required if the service were provided in person or by other means.

4. The provisions of this section do not require an insurer to:

(a) Ensure that covered services are available to an insured through telehealth at a particular originating site;

(b) Provide coverage for a service that is not a covered service or that is not provided by a covered provider of health care; or

(c) Enter into a contract with any provider of health care or cover any service if the insurer is not otherwise required by law to do so.

5. A policy of health insurance subject to the provisions of this chapter that is delivered, issued for delivery or renewed on or after July 1, 2015, has the legal effect of including the coverage required by this section, and any provision of the policy or the renewal which is in conflict with this section is void.

6. As used in this section:

(a) "Distant site" has the meaning ascribed to it in NRS 629.515.

(b) "Originating site" has the meaning ascribed to it in NRS 629.515.

(c) "Provider of health care" has the meaning ascribed to it in NRS 439.820.

(d) "Telehealth" has the meaning ascribed to it in NRS 629.515.

NRS 689B.0369

Required provision concerning coverage for services provided through telehealth

1. A policy of group or blanket health insurance must include coverage for services provided to an insured through telehealth to the same extent as though provided in person or by other means.

2. An insurer shall not:

(a) Require an insured to establish a relationship in person with a provider of health care or provide any additional consent to or reason for obtaining services through telehealth as a condition to providing the coverage described in subsection 1;

(b) Require a provider of health care to demonstrate that it is necessary to provide services to an insured through telehealth or receive any additional type of certification or license to provide services through telehealth as a condition to providing the coverage described in subsection 1;

(c) Refuse to provide the coverage described in subsection 1 because of the distant site from which a provider of health care provides services through telehealth or the originating site at which an insured receives services through telehealth; or

(d) Require covered services to be provided through telehealth as a condition to providing coverage for such services.

3. A policy of group or blanket health insurance must not require an insured to obtain prior authorization for any service provided through telehealth that is not required for that service when provided in person. A policy of group or blanket health insurance may require prior authorization for a service provided through telehealth if such prior authorization would be required if the service were provided in person or by other means.

4. The provisions of this section do not require an insurer to:

(a) Ensure that covered services are available to an insured through telehealth at a particular originating site;

(b) Provide coverage for a service that is not a covered service or that is not provided by a covered provider of health care; or

(c) Enter into a contract with any provider of health care or cover any service if the insurer is not otherwise required by law to do so.

5. A policy of group or blanket health insurance subject to the provisions of this chapter that is delivered, issued for delivery or renewed on or after July 1, 2015, has the legal effect of including the coverage required by this section, and any provision of the policy or the renewal which is in conflict with this section is void.

6. As used in this section:

(a) "Distant site" has the meaning ascribed to it in NRS 629.515.

(b) "Originating site" has the meaning ascribed to it in NRS 629.515.

(c) "Provider of health care" has the meaning ascribed to it in NRS 439.820.

(d) "Telehealth" has the meaning ascribed to it in NRS 629.515.

NRS 616C.730

Policy of insurance required to include coverage for services provided through telehealth; limitations

1. Every policy of insurance issued pursuant to chapters 616A to 617, inclusive, of NRS must include coverage for services provided to an employee through telehealth to the same extent as though provided in person or by other means.

2. An insurer shall not:

(a) Require an employee to establish a relationship in person with a provider of health care or provide any additional consent to or reason for obtaining services through telehealth as a condition to providing the coverage described in subsection 1;

(b) Require a provider of health care to demonstrate that it is necessary to provide services to an employee through telehealth or receive any additional type of certification or license to provide services through telehealth as a condition to providing the coverage described in subsection 1;

(c) Refuse to provide the coverage described in subsection 1 because of the distant site from which a provider of health care provides services through telehealth or the originating site at which an employee receives services through telehealth; or

(d) Require covered services to be provided through telehealth as a condition to providing coverage for such services.

3. A policy of insurance issued pursuant to chapters 616A to 617, inclusive, of NRS must not require an employee to obtain prior authorization for any service provided through telehealth that is not required for the service when provided in person. Such a policy of insurance may require prior authorization for a service provided through telehealth if such prior authorization would be required if the service were provided in person or by other means.

4. The provisions of this section do not require an insurer to:

(a) Ensure that covered services are available to an employee through telehealth at a particular originating site;

(b) Provide coverage for a service that is not a covered service or that is not provided by a covered provider of health care; or

(c) Enter into a contract with any provider of health care or cover any service if the insurer is not otherwise required by law to do so.

5. A policy of insurance subject to the provisions of chapters 616A to 617, inclusive, of NRS that is delivered, issued for delivery or renewed on or after July 1, 2015, has the legal effect of including the coverage required by this section, and any provision of the policy or the renewal which is in conflict with this section is void.

6. As used in this section:

(a) "Distant site" has the meaning ascribed to it in NRS 629.515.

(b) "Originating site" has the meaning ascribed to it in NRS 629.515.

(c) "Provider of health care" has the meaning ascribed to it in NRS 439.820.

(d) "Telehealth" has the meaning ascribed to it in NRS 629.515.

NRS 695D.216

Required provision concerning coverage for services provided through telehealth

1. A plan for dental care must include coverage for services provided to a member through telehealth to the same extent as though provided in person or by other means.

2. An organization for dental care shall not:

(a) Require a member to establish a relationship in person with a provider of health care or provide any additional consent to or reason for obtaining services through telehealth as a condition to providing the coverage described in subsection 1;

(b) Require a provider of health care to demonstrate that it is necessary to provide services to a member through telehealth or receive any additional type of certification or license to provide services through telehealth as a condition to providing the coverage described in subsection 1;

(c) Refuse to provide the coverage described in subsection 1 because of the distant site from which a provider of health care provides services through telehealth or the originating site at which a member receives services through telehealth; or

(d) Require covered services to be provided through telehealth as a condition to providing coverage for such services.

3. A plan for dental care must not require a member to obtain prior authorization for any service provided through telehealth that is not required for the service when provided in person. A plan for dental care may require prior authorization for a service provided through telehealth if such prior authorization would be required if the service were provided in person or by other means.

4. The provisions of this section do not require an organization for dental care to:

(a) Ensure that covered services are available to a member through telehealth at a particular originating site;

(b) Provide coverage for a service that is not a covered service or that is not provided by a covered provider of health care; or

(c) Enter into a contract with any provider of health care or cover any service if the organization for dental care is not otherwise required by law to do so.

5. A plan for dental care subject to the provisions of this chapter that is delivered, issued for delivery or renewed on or after July 1, 2015, has the legal effect of including the coverage required by this section, and any provision of the plan or the renewal which is in conflict with this section is void.

6. As used in this section:

(a) "Distant site" has the meaning ascribed to it in NRS 629.515.

(b) "Originating site" has the meaning ascribed to it in NRS 629.515.

(c) "Provider of health care" has the meaning ascribed to it in NRS 439.820.

(d) "Telehealth" has the meaning ascribed to it in NRS 629.515.

NRS 695C.1708

Required provision concerning coverage for services provided through telehealth

1. A health care plan of a health maintenance organization must include coverage for services provided to an enrollee through telehealth to the same extent as though provided in person or by other means.

2. A health maintenance organization shall not:

(a) Require an enrollee to establish a relationship in person with a provider of health care or provide any additional consent to or reason for obtaining services through telehealth as a condition to providing the coverage described in subsection 1;

(b) Require a provider of health care to demonstrate that it is necessary to provide services to an enrollee through telehealth or receive any additional type of certification or license to provide services through telehealth as a condition to providing the coverage described in subsection 1;

(c) Refuse to provide the coverage described in subsection 1 because of the distant site from which a provider of health care provides services through telehealth or the originating site at which an enrollee receives services through telehealth; or

(d) Require covered services to be provided through telehealth as a condition to providing coverage for such services.

3. A health care plan of a health maintenance organization must not require an enrollee to obtain prior authorization for any service provided through telehealth that is not required for the service when provided in person. Such a health care plan may require prior authorization for a service

provided through telehealth if such prior authorization would be required if the service were provided in person or by other means.

4. The provisions of this section do not require a health maintenance organization to:

(a) Ensure that covered services are available to an enrollee through telehealth at a particular originating site;

(b) Provide coverage for a service that is not a covered service or that is not provided by a covered provider of health care; or

(c) Enter into a contract with any provider of health care or cover any service if the health maintenance organization is not otherwise required by law to do so.

5. Evidence of coverage subject to the provisions of this chapter that is delivered, issued for delivery or renewed on or after July 1, 2015, has the legal effect of including the coverage required by this section, and any provision of the plan or the renewal which is in conflict with this section is void.

6. As used in this section:

(a) "Distant site" has the meaning ascribed to it in NRS 629.515.

(b) "Originating site" has the meaning ascribed to it in NRS 629.515.

(c) "Provider of health care" has the meaning ascribed to it in NRS 439.820.

(d) "Telehealth" has the meaning ascribed to it in NRS 629.515.

NRS 695G.162

Required provision concerning coverage for services provided through telehealth

1. A health care plan issued by a managed care organization for group coverage must include coverage for services provided to an insured through telehealth to the same extent as though provided in person or by other means.

2. A managed care organization shall not:

(a) Require an insured to establish a relationship in person with a provider of health care or provide any additional consent to or reason for obtaining services through telehealth as a condition to providing the coverage described in subsection 1;

(b) Require a provider of health care to demonstrate that it is necessary to provide services to an insured through telehealth or receive any additional type of certification or license to provide services through telehealth as a condition to providing the coverage described in subsection 1;

(c) Refuse to provide the coverage described in subsection 1 because of the distant site from which a provider of health care provides services through telehealth or the originating site at which an insured receives services through telehealth; or

(d) Require covered services to be provided through telehealth as a condition to providing coverage for such services.

3. A health care plan of a managed care organization must not require an insured to obtain prior authorization for any service provided through telehealth that is not required for the service when provided in person. Such a health care plan may require prior authorization for a service provided through telehealth if such prior authorization would be required if the service were provided in person or by other means.

4. The provisions of this section do not require a managed care organization to:

(a) Ensure that covered services are available to an insured through telehealth at a particular originating site;

(b) Provide coverage for a service that is not a covered service or that is not provided by a covered provider of health care; or

(c) Enter into a contract with any provider of health care or cover any service if the managed care organization is not otherwise required by law to do so.

5. Evidence of coverage that is delivered, issued for delivery or renewed on or after July 1, 2015, has the legal effect of including the coverage required by this section, and any provision of the plan or the renewal which is in conflict with this section is void.

6. As used in this section:

(a) "Distant site" has the meaning ascribed to it in NRS 629.515.

(b) "Originating site" has the meaning ascribed to it in NRS 629.515.

(c) "Provider of health care" has the meaning ascribed to it in NRS 439.820.

(d) "Telehealth" has the meaning ascribed to it in NRS 629.515.

NRS 695B.1904

Required provision concerning coverage for services provided through telehealth

1. A contract for hospital, medical or dental services subject to the provisions of this chapter must include services provided to an insured through telehealth to the same extent as though provided in person or by other means.

2. A medical services corporation that issues contracts for hospital, medical or dental services shall not:

(a) Require an insured to establish a relationship in person with a provider of health care or provide any additional consent to or reason for obtaining services through telehealth as a condition to providing the coverage described in subsection 1;

(b) Require a provider of health care to demonstrate that it is necessary to provide services to an insured through telehealth or receive any additional type of certification or license to provide services through telehealth as a condition to providing the coverage described in subsection 1;

(c) Refuse to provide the coverage described in subsection 1 because of the distant site from which a provider of health care provides services through telehealth or the originating site at which an insured receives services through telehealth; or

(d) Require covered services to be provided through telehealth as a condition to providing coverage for such services.

3. A contract for hospital, medical or dental services must not require an insured to obtain prior authorization for any service provided through telehealth that is not required for the service when provided in person. A contract for hospital, medical or dental services may require prior authorization for a service provided through telehealth if such prior authorization would be required if the service were provided in person or by other means.

4. The provisions of this section do not require a medical services corporation that issues contracts for hospital, medical or dental services to:

(a) Ensure that covered services are available to an insured through telehealth at a particular originating site;

(b) Provide coverage for a service that is not a covered service or that is not provided by a covered provider of health care; or

(c) Enter into a contract with any provider of health care or cover any service if the medical services corporation is not otherwise required by law to do so.

5. A contract for hospital, medical or dental services subject to the provisions of this chapter that is delivered, issued for delivery or renewed on or after July 1, 2015, has the legal effect of

including the coverage required by this section, and any provision of the contract or the renewal which is in conflict with this section is void.

6. As used in this section:

(a) "Distant site" has the meaning ascribed to it in NRS 629.515.

(b) "Originating site" has the meaning ascribed to it in NRS 629.515.

(c) "Provider of health care" has the meaning ascribed to it in NRS 439.820.

(d) "Telehealth" has the meaning ascribed to it in NRS 629.515.

NEW HAMPSHIRE

N.H. Rev. Stat. § 415-J:3

Coverage for Telemedicine Services

I. It is the intent of the general court to recognize the application of telemedicine for covered services provided within the scope of practice of a physician or other health care provider as a method of delivery of medical care by which an individual shall receive medical services from a health care provider without in-person contact with the provider.

II. An insurer offering a health plan in this state may not deny coverage on the sole basis that the coverage is provided through telemedicine if the health care service would be covered if it were provided through in-person consultation between the covered person and a health care provider.

III. Nothing in this section shall be construed to prohibit an insurer from providing coverage for only those services that are medically necessary and subject to the terms and conditions of the covered person's policy.

NEW JERSEY

(NONE)

NEW MEXICO

NMSA 1978, § 59A-46-50.3

Coverage for telemedicine services

A. An individual or group health maintenance organization contract that is delivered, issued for delivery or renewed in this state shall allow covered benefits to be provided through telemedicine services. Coverage for health care services provided through telemedicine shall be determined in a manner consistent with coverage for health care services provided through in-person consultation.

B. The provisions of this section shall not be construed to require coverage of an otherwise non-covered benefit.

C. A determination by a health maintenance organization that health care services delivered through the use of telemedicine are not covered under the plan shall be subject to review and appeal pursuant to the Patient Protection Act.

D. The provisions of this section shall not apply in the event that federal law requires the state to make payments on behalf of enrollees to cover the costs of implementing this section.

E. Nothing in this section shall require a health care provider to be physically present with a patient at the originating site unless the consulting telemedicine provider deems it necessary.

F. Telemedicine used to provide clinical services shall be encrypted and shall conform to state and federal privacy laws.

G. The provisions of this section shall not apply to an individual or group health maintenance organization contract intended to supplement major medical group-type coverage, such as Medicare supplement, long-term care, disability income, specified disease, accident-only, hospital indemnity or any other limited-benefit health insurance policy.

H. As used in this section:

(1) "consulting telemedicine provider" means a health care provider that delivers telemedicine services from a location remote from an originating site;

(2) "in real time" means occurring simultaneously, instantaneously or within seconds of an event so that there is little or no noticeable delay between two or more events;

(3) "originating site" means a place at which a patient is physically located and receiving health care services via telemedicine;

(4) "store-and-forward technology" means electronic information, imaging and communication, including interactive audio, video and data communication, that is transferred or recorded or otherwise stored for asynchronous use; and

(5) "telemedicine" means the use of interactive simultaneous audio and video or store-and-forward technology using information and telecommunications technologies by a health care provider to deliver health care services within that provider's scope of practice at a site other than the site where the patient is located, including the use of electronic media for consultation relating to the health care diagnosis or treatment of the patient in real time or through the use of store-and-forward technology.

NMSA 1978, § 59A-23-7.12

Coverage for telemedicine services

A. A blanket or group health insurance policy or contract that is delivered, issued for delivery or renewed in this state shall allow covered benefits to be provided through telemedicine services. Coverage for health care services provided through telemedicine shall be determined in a manner consistent with coverage for health care services provided through in-person consultation.

B. The provisions of this section shall not be construed to require coverage of an otherwise non-covered benefit.

C. A determination by an insurer that health care services delivered through the use of telemedicine are not covered under the plan shall be subject to review and appeal pursuant to the Patient Protection Act.

D. The provisions of this section shall not apply in the event that federal law requires the state to make payments on behalf of enrollees to cover the costs of implementing this section.

E. Nothing in this section shall require a health care provider to be physically present with a patient at the originating site unless the consulting telemedicine provider deems it necessary.

F. Telemedicine used to provide clinical services shall be encrypted and shall conform to state and federal privacy laws.

G. The provisions of this section shall not apply to a group or blanket policy, plan or contract intended to supplement major medical group-type coverage, such as Medicare supplement, long-term care, disability income, specified disease, accident-only, hospital indemnity or any other limited-benefit health insurance policy.

H. As used in this section:

(1) "consulting telemedicine provider" means a health care provider that delivers telemedicine services from a location remote from an originating site;

(2) "health care provider" means a duly licensed hospital or other licensed facility, physician or other health care professional authorized to furnish health care services within the scope of the professional's license;

(3) "in real time" means occurring simultaneously, instantaneously or within seconds of an event so that there is little or no noticeable delay between two or more events;

(4) "originating site" means a place at which a patient is physically located and receiving health care services via telemedicine;

(5) "store-and-forward technology" means electronic information, imaging and communication, including interactive audio, video and data communication, that is transferred or recorded or otherwise stored for asynchronous use; and

(6) "telemedicine" means the use of interactive simultaneous audio and video or store-and-forward technology using information and telecommunications technologies by a health care provider to deliver health care services at a site other than the site where the patient is located, including the use of electronic media for consultation relating to the health care diagnosis or treatment of the patient in real time or through the use of store-and-forward technology.

NMSA 1978, § 59A-22-49.3

Coverage for telemedicine services

A. An individual or group health insurance policy, health care plan or certificate of health insurance that is delivered, issued for delivery or renewed in this state shall allow covered benefits to be provided through telemedicine services. Coverage for health care services provided through telemedicine shall be determined in a manner consistent with coverage for health care services provided through in-person consultation.

B. The provisions of this section shall not be construed to require coverage of an otherwise non-covered benefit.

C. A determination by an insurer that health care services delivered through the use of telemedicine are not covered under the plan shall be subject to review and appeal pursuant to the Patient Protection Act.

D. The provisions of this section shall not apply in the event that federal law requires the state to make payments on behalf of enrollees to cover the costs of implementing this section.

E. Nothing in this section shall require a health care provider to be physically present with a patient at the originating site unless the consulting telemedicine provider deems it necessary.

F. Telemedicine used to provide clinical services shall be encrypted and shall conform to state and federal privacy laws.

G. The provisions of this section shall not apply to an individual policy, plan or contract intended to supplement major medical group-type coverage, such as Medicare supplement, long-term care, disability income, specified disease, accident-only, hospital indemnity or any other limited-benefit health insurance policy.

H. As used in this section:

(1) "consulting telemedicine provider" means a health care provider that delivers telemedicine services from a location remote from an originating site;

(2) "health care provider" means a duly licensed hospital or other licensed facility, physician or other health care professional authorized to furnish health care services within the scope of the professional's license;

(3) "in real time" means occurring simultaneously, instantaneously or within seconds of an event so that there is little or no noticeable delay between two or more events;

(4) "originating site" means a place at which a patient is physically located and receiving health care services via telemedicine;

(5) "store-and-forward technology" means electronic information, imaging and communication, including interactive audio, video and data communication, that is transferred or recorded or otherwise stored for asynchronous use; and

(6) "telemedicine" means the use of interactive simultaneous audio and video or store-and-

forward technology using information and telecommunications technologies by a health care provider to deliver health care services at a site other than the site where the patient is located, including the use of electronic media for consultation relating to the health care diagnosis or treatment of the patient in real time or through the use of store-and-forward technology.

NMSA 1978, § 59A-47-45.3

Coverage for telemedicine services

A. An individual or group health insurance policy, health care plan or certificate of health insurance delivered or issued for delivery in this state shall allow covered benefits to be provided through telemedicine services. Coverage for health care services provided through telemedicine shall be determined in a manner consistent with coverage for health care services provided through in-person consultation.

B. The provisions of this section shall not be construed to require coverage of an otherwise non-covered benefit.

C. A determination by a nonprofit health plan that health care services delivered through the use of telemedicine are not covered under the plan shall be subject to review and appeal pursuant to the Patient Protection Act.

D. The provisions of this section shall not apply in the event that federal law requires the state to make payments on behalf of enrollees to cover the costs of implementing this section.

E. Nothing in this section shall require a health care provider to be physically present with a patient at the originating site unless the consulting telemedicine provider deems it necessary.

F. Telemedicine used to provide clinical services shall be encrypted and shall conform to state and federal privacy laws.

G. The provisions of this section shall not apply to an individual or group health care plan intended to supplement major medical group-type coverage, such as Medicare supplement, long-term care, disability income, specified disease, accident-only, hospital indemnity or any other limited-benefit health insurance policy.

H. As used in this section:

(1) "consulting telemedicine provider" means a health care provider that delivers telemedicine services from a location remote from an originating site;

(2) "health care provider" means a duly licensed hospital or other licensed facility, physician or other health care professional authorized to furnish health care services within the scope of the professional's license;

(3) "in real time" means occurring simultaneously, instantaneously or within seconds of an event so that there is little or no noticeable delay between two or more events;

(4) "originating site" means a place at which a patient is physically located and receiving health care services via telemedicine;

(5) "store-and-forward technology" means electronic information, imaging and communication, including interactive audio, video and data communication, that is transferred or recorded or otherwise stored for asynchronous use; and

(6) "telemedicine" means the use of interactive simultaneous audio and video or store-and-forward technology using information and telecommunications technologies by a health care provider to deliver health care services at a site other than the site where the patient is located, including the use of electronic media for consultation relating to the health care diagnosis or treatment of the patient in real time or through the use of store-and-forward technology.

NEW YORK

NY Ins. Law § 3217-h

Telehealth delivery of services

(a) An insurer shall not exclude from coverage a service that is otherwise covered under a policy that provides comprehensive coverage for hospital, medical or surgical care because the service is delivered via telehealth, as that term is defined in subsection (b) of this section; provided, however, that an insurer may exclude from coverage a service by a health care provider where the provider is not otherwise covered under the policy. An insurer may subject the coverage of a service delivered via telehealth to copayments, coinsurance or deductibles provided that they are at least as favorable to the insured as those established for the same service when not delivered via telehealth. An insurer may subject the coverage of a service delivered via telehealth to reasonable utilization management and quality assurance requirements that are consistent with those established for the same service when not delivered via telehealth.

(b) For purposes of this section, "telehealth" means the use of electronic information and communication technologies by a health care provider to deliver health care services to an insured individual while such individual is located at a site that is different from the site where the health care provider is located.

NY Ins. Law § 4406-g

Telehealth delivery of services

1. A health maintenance organization shall not exclude from coverage a service that is otherwise covered under an enrollee contract of a health maintenance organization because the service is delivered via telehealth, as that term is defined in subdivision two of this section; provided, however, that a health maintenance organization may exclude from coverage a service by a health care provider where the provider is not otherwise covered under the enrollee contract. A health maintenance organization may subject the coverage of a service delivered via telehealth to copayments, coinsurance or deductibles provided that they are at least as favorable to the enrollee as those established for the same service when not delivered via telehealth. A health maintenance organization may subject the coverage of a service delivered via telehealth to reasonable utilization management and quality assurance requirements that are consistent with those established for the same service when not delivered via telehealth.

2. For purposes of this section, "telehealth" means the use of electronic information and communication technologies by a health care provider to deliver health care services to an enrollee while such enrollee is located at a site that is different from the site where the health care provider is located.

NY Ins. Law § 4306-g

Telehealth delivery of services

(a) A corporation shall not exclude from coverage a service that is otherwise covered under a contract that provides comprehensive coverage for hospital, medical or surgical care because the service is delivered via telehealth, as that term is defined in subsection (b) of this section; provided, however, that a corporation may exclude from coverage a service by a health care provider where the provider is not otherwise covered under the contract. A corporation may subject the coverage of a service delivered via telehealth to copayments, coinsurance or deductibles provided that they are at least as favorable to the insured as those established for the same service when not delivered via telehealth. A corporation may subject the coverage of a service delivered via telehealth to reasonable utilization management and quality assurance requirements that are consistent with those established for the same service when not delivered via telehealth.

(b) For purposes of this section, "telehealth" means the use of electronic information and communication technologies by a health care provider to deliver health care services to an insured individual while such individual is located at a site that is different from the site where the health care provider is located.

NY Pub. Health Law § 2999-dd.

Telehealth delivery of services

Health care services delivered by means of telehealth shall be entitled to reimbursement under section three hundred sixty-seven-u of the social services law.

NORTH CAROLINA
(NONE)

NORTH DAKOTA
(NONE)

OHIO
(NONE)

OKLAHOMA

36 Okl. St. Ann. § 6803

Coverage of telemedicine services

A. Services that a health care practitioner determines to be appropriately provided by means of telemedicine, health care service plans, disability insurer programs, workers' compensation programs or state Medicaid managed care program contracts issued, amended or renewed on or after January 1, 1998, shall not require person-to-person contact between a health care practitioner and a patient.

B. Subsection A of this section shall apply to health care service plan contracts with the state Medicaid managed care program only to the extent that both of the following apply:

1. Telemedicine services are covered by, and reimbursed under, the fee-for-service provisions of the state Medicaid managed care program; and

2. State Medicaid managed care program contracts with health care service plans are amended to add coverage of telemedicine services and make any appropriate capitation rate adjustments.

OREGON

ORS § 743A.058

Coverage of health service provided using synchronous two-way interactive video conferencing

(1) As used in this section:

(a) "Health benefit plan" includes:

(A) A health benefit plan as defined in ORS 743B.005; and

(B) A self-insured health plan offered through the Public Employees' Benefit Board or the Oregon Educators Benefit Board.

(b) "Health professional" means a person licensed, certified or registered in this state to provide health care services or supplies.

(c) "Originating site" means the physical location of the patient.

(2) A health benefit plan must provide coverage of a health service that is provided using synchronous two-way interactive video conferencing if:

(a) The plan provides coverage of the health service when provided in person by a health professional;

(b) The health service is medically necessary;

(c) The health service is determined to be safely and effectively provided using synchronous two-way interactive video conferencing according to generally accepted health care practices and standards; and

(d) The application and technology used to provide the health service meet all standards required by state and federal laws governing the privacy and security of protected health information.

(3) A health benefit plan may not distinguish between rural and urban originating sites in providing coverage under subsection (2) of this section.

(4) The coverage under subsection (2) of this section is subject to:

(a) The terms and conditions of the health benefit plan; and

(b) The reimbursement specified in the contract between the plan and the health professional.

(5) This section does not require a health benefit plan to reimburse a health professional:

(a) For a health service that is not a covered benefit under the plan; or

(b) Who has not contracted with the plan.

PENNSYLVANIA
(NONE)

RHODE ISLAND

Gen. Laws 1956, § 27-81-4

Coverage of telemedicine services

(a) Each health insurer that issues individual or group accident and sickness insurance policies for health care services and/or provides a health care plan for health care services shall provide coverage for the cost of such covered health care services provided through telemedicine services, as provided in this section.

(b) A health insurer shall not exclude a health care service for coverage solely because the health care service is provided through telemedicine and is not provided through in-person consultation or contact, so long as such health care services are medically appropriate to be provided through telemedicine services and, as such, may be subject to the terms and conditions of a telemedicine agreement between the insurer and the participating health care provider or provider group.

(c) Benefit plans offered by a health insurer may impose a deductible, copayment or coinsurance requirement for a health care service provided through telemedicine.

(d) The requirements of this section shall apply to all policies and health plans issued, reissued or delivered in the state of Rhode Island on and after January 1, 2018.

(e) This chapter shall not apply to: short-term travel, accident-only, limited or specified disease; or individual conversion policies or health plans; nor to policies or health plans designed for issuance to persons eligible for coverage under Title XVIII of the Social Security Act, known as Medicare; or any other similar coverage under state or federal governmental plans.

SOUTH CAROLINA
(NONE)

SOUTH DAKOTA
(NONE)

TENNESSEE

TCA § 56-7-1002

Health care services delivered through telehealth encounter

(a) As used in this section:

(1) "Health insurance entity" has the same meaning as defined in § 56-7-109 and includes managed care organizations participating in the medical assistance program under Title 71, chapter 5;

(2) "Health care services" has the same meaning as defined in § 56-61-102;

(3) "Health care services provider" means an individual acting within the scope of a valid license issued pursuant to title 63 or any state-contracted crisis service provider employed by a facility licensed under Title 33;

(4) "Qualified site" means the office of a health care services provider, a hospital licensed under Title 68, a facility recognized as a rural health clinic under federal Medicare regulations, a federally qualified health center, any facility licensed under Title 33, or any other location deemed acceptable by the health insurance entity;

(5) "Store-and-forward telemedicine services":

(A) Means the use of asynchronous computer-based communications between a patient and health care services provider at a distant site for the purpose of diagnostic and therapeutic assistance in the care of patients; and

(B) Includes the transferring of medical data from one (1) site to another through the use of a camera or similar device that records or stores an image that is sent or forwarded via telecommunication to another site for consultation;

(6) "Telehealth":

(A) Means the use of real-time, interactive audio, video telecommunications or electronic technology or store-and-forward telemedicine services by a health care services provider to deliver health care services to a patient within the scope of practice of the health care services provider when:

(i) Such provider is at a qualified site other than the site where the patient is located; and

(ii) The patient is at a qualified site or at a school clinic staffed by a health care services provider and equipped to engage in the telecommunications described in this section; and

(B) Does not include:

(i) An audio-only conversation;

(ii) An electronic mail message; or

(iii) A facsimile transmission; and

(7) "Telehealth provider" means a health care services provider engaged in the delivery of health care services through telehealth.

(b) Health care services provided through a telehealth encounter shall comply with state licensure requirements promulgated by the appropriate licensure boards. Telehealth providers shall be held to the same standard of care as health care services providers providing the same health care service through in-person encounters.

(c) A telehealth provider who seeks to contract with or who has contracted with a health insurance entity to participate in the health insurance entity's network shall be subject to the same requirements and contractual terms as a health care services provider in the health insurance entity's network.

(d) Subject to subsection (c), a health insurance entity:

(1) Shall provide coverage under a health insurance policy or contract for covered health care services delivered through telehealth;

(2) Shall reimburse a health care services provider for the diagnosis, consultation and treatment of an insured patient for a health care service covered under a health insurance policy

or contract that is provided through telehealth without any distinction or consideration of the geographic location or any federal, state or local designation, or classification of the geographic area where the patient is located;

(3) Shall not exclude from coverage a health care service solely because it is provided through telehealth and is not provided through an in-person encounter between a health care services provider and a patient; and

(4) Shall reimburse health care services providers who are out-of-network for telehealth care services under the same reimbursement policies applicable to other out-of-network health care services providers.

(e) A health insurance entity shall provide coverage for health care services provided during a telehealth encounter in a manner that is consistent with what the health insurance policy or contract provides for in-person encounters for the same service, and shall reimburse for health care services provided during a telehealth encounter without distinction or consideration of the geographic location, or any federal, state or local designation or classification of the geographic area where the patient is located.

(f) Nothing in this section shall require a health insurance entity to pay total reimbursement for a telehealth encounter, including the use of telehealth equipment, in an amount that exceeds the amount that would be paid for the same service provided by a health care services provider in an in-person encounter.

(g) Any provisions not stipulated by this section shall be governed by the terms and conditions of the health insurance contract.

(h) Nothing in this section shall apply to accident-only, specified disease, hospital indemnity, plans described in § 1251 of the Patient Protection and Affordable Care Act, Public Law 111-148, as amended and § 2301 of the Health Care and Education Reconciliation Act of 2010, Public Law 111-152, as amended (both in 42 U.S.C. § 18011), plans described in the Employee Retirement Income Security Act of 1974 (ERISA) (29 U.S.C. § 1001 *et seq.*), Medicare supplement, disability income, long-term care or other limited benefit hospital insurance policies.

TEXAS

VTCA, Insurance Code § 1455.004

Coverage for Telemedicine Medical Services and Telehealth Services

(a) A health benefit plan may not exclude a telemedicine medical service or a telehealth service from coverage under the plan solely because the service is not provided through a face-to-face consultation.

(b) A health benefit plan may require a deductible, a copayment or coinsurance for a telemedicine medical service or a telehealth service. The amount of the deductible, copayment or coinsurance may not exceed the amount of the deductible, copayment or coinsurance required for a comparable medical service provided through a face-to-face consultation.

UTAH

(NONE)

VERMONT

8 VSA § 4100k

Coverage of telemedicine services

(a) All health insurance plans in this State shall provide coverage for telemedicine services delivered to a patient in a health care facility to the same extent that the services would be covered if they were provided through in-person consultation.

(b) A health insurance plan may charge a deductible, copayment or coinsurance for a health care service provided through telemedicine so long as it does not exceed the deductible, copayment or coinsurance applicable to an in-person consultation.

(c) A health insurance plan may limit coverage to health care providers in the plan's network and may require originating site health care providers to document the reason the services are being provided by telemedicine rather than in person.

(d) Nothing in this section shall be construed to prohibit a health insurance plan from providing coverage for only those services that are medically necessary, subject to the terms and conditions of the covered person's policy.

(e) A health insurance plan may reimburse for teleophthalmology or teledermatology provided by store and forward means and may require the distant site health care provider to document the reason the services are being provided by store and forward means.

(f) Nothing in this section shall be construed to require a health insurance plan to reimburse the distant site health care provider if the distant site health care provider has insufficient information to render an opinion.

(g) In order to facilitate the use of telemedicine in treating substance use disorder, health insurers and the Department of Vermont Health Access shall ensure that both the treating clinician and the hosting facility are reimbursed for the services rendered, unless the health care providers at both the host and service sites are employed by the same entity.

(h) As used in this subchapter:

(1) "Health insurance plan" means any health insurance policy or health benefit plan offered by a health insurer, as defined in 18 V.S.A. § 9402, as well as Medicaid and any other public health care assistance program offered or administered by the State or by any subdivision or instrumentality of the State. The term does not include policies or plans providing coverage for a specified disease or other limited-benefit coverage.

(2) "Health care facility" shall have the same meaning as in 18 V.S.A. § 9402.

(3) "Store and forward" means an asynchronous transmission of medical information to be reviewed at a later date by a health care provider at a distant site who is trained in the relevant specialty and by which the health care provider at the distant site reviews the medical information without the patient present in real time.

(4) "Telemedicine" means the delivery of health care services such as diagnosis, consultation or treatment through the use of live interactive audio and video over a secure connection that complies with the requirements of the Health Insurance Portability and Accountability Act of 1996, Public Law 104-191. Telemedicine does not include the use of audio-only telephone, e-mail or facsimile.

VIRGINIA

VA Code Ann. § 38.2-3418.16

Coverage for telemedicine services

A. Notwithstanding the provisions of § 38.2-3419, each insurer proposing to issue individual or group accident and sickness insurance policies providing hospital, medical and surgical, or major medical coverage on an expense-incurred basis; each corporation providing individual or group accident and sickness subscription contracts; and each health maintenance organization providing a health care plan for health care services shall provide coverage for the cost of such health care services provided through telemedicine services, as provided in this section.

B. As used in this section, "telemedicine services," as it pertains to the delivery of health care services, means the use of electronic technology or media, including interactive audio or video, for the purpose of diagnosing or treating a patient or consulting with other health care providers regarding a patient's diagnosis or treatment." Telemedicine services" does not include an audio-only telephone, electronic mail message, facsimile transmission or online questionnaire.

C. An insurer, corporation or health maintenance organization shall not exclude a service for coverage solely because the service is provided through telemedicine services and is not provided through face-to-face consultation or contact between a health care provider and a patient for services appropriately provided through telemedicine services.

D. An insurer, corporation or health maintenance organization shall not be required to reimburse the treating provider or the consulting provider for technical fees or costs for the provision of telemedicine services; however, such insurer, corporation or health maintenance organization shall reimburse the treating provider or the consulting provider for the diagnosis, consultation or treatment of the insured delivered through telemedicine services on the same basis that the insurer, corporation or health maintenance organization is responsible for coverage for the provision of the same service through face-to-face consultation or contact.

E. Nothing shall preclude the insurer, corporation or health maintenance organization from undertaking utilization review to determine the appropriateness of telemedicine services, provided that such appropriateness is made in the same manner as those determinations are made for the treatment of any other illness, condition or disorder covered by such policy, contract or plan. Any such utilization review shall not require pre-authorization of emergent telemedicine services.

F. An insurer, corporation or health maintenance organization may offer a health plan containing a deductible, copayment or coinsurance requirement for a health care service provided through telemedicine services, provided that the deductible, copayment or coinsurance does not exceed the deductible, copayment or coinsurance applicable if the same services were provided through face-to-face diagnosis, consultation or treatment.

G. No insurer, corporation or health maintenance organization shall impose any annual or lifetime dollar maximum on coverage for telemedicine services other than an annual or lifetime dollar maximum that applies in the aggregate to all items and services covered under the policy, or impose upon any person receiving benefits pursuant to this section any copayment, coinsurance or deductible amounts, or any policy year, calendar year, lifetime or other durational benefit limitation or maximum for benefits or services, that is not equally imposed upon all terms and services covered under the policy, contract or plan.

H. The requirements of this section shall apply to all insurance policies, contracts and plans delivered, issued for delivery, reissued or extended in the Commonwealth on and after January 1, 2011, or at any time thereafter when any term of the policy, contract or plan is changed or any premium adjustment is made.

I. This section shall not apply to short-term travel, accident-only or limited or specified disease policies or contracts, nor to policies or contracts designed for issuance to persons eligible for coverage under Title XVIII of the Social Security Act, known as Medicare, or any other similar coverage under state or federal governmental plans.

WASHINGTON

RCWA 48.43.735

Reimbursement of health care services provided through telemedicine or store and forward technology

(1) For health plans issued or renewed on or after January 1, 2017, a health carrier shall reimburse a provider for a health care service provided to a covered person through telemedicine or store and forward technology if:

(a) The plan provides coverage of the health care service when provided in person by the provider;

(b) The health care service is medically necessary;

(c) The health care service is a service recognized as an essential health benefit under section 1302(b) of the federal Patient Protection and Affordable Care Act in effect on January 1, 2015; and

(d) The health care service is determined to be safely and effectively provided through telemedicine or store and forward technology according to generally accepted health care practices and standards, and the technology used to provide the health care service meets the standards required by state and federal laws governing the privacy and security of protected health information.

(2) (a) If the service is provided through store and forward technology there must be an associated office visit between the covered person and the referring health care provider. Nothing in this section prohibits the use of telemedicine for the associated office visit.

(b) For purposes of this section, reimbursement of store and forward technology is available only for those covered services specified in the negotiated agreement between the health carrier and the health care provider.

(3) An originating site for a telemedicine health care service subject to subsection (1) of this section includes a:

(a) Hospital;

(b) Rural health clinic;

(c) Federally qualified health center;

(d) Physician's or other health care provider's office;

(e) Community mental health center;

(f) Skilled nursing facility;

(g) Home; or

(h) Renal dialysis center, except an independent renal dialysis center.

(4) Except for subsection (3)(g) of this section, any originating site under subsection (3) of this section may charge a facility fee for infrastructure and preparation of the patient. Reimbursement must be subject to a negotiated agreement between the originating site and the health carrier. A distant site or any other site not identified in subsection (3) of this section may not charge a facility fee.

(5) A health carrier may not distinguish between originating sites that are rural and urban in providing the coverage required in subsection (1) of this section.

(6) A health carrier may subject coverage of a telemedicine or store and forward technology health service under subsection (1) of this section to all terms and conditions of the plan in which the covered person is enrolled, including, but not limited to, utilization review, prior authorization, deductible, copayment or coinsurance requirements that are applicable to coverage of a comparable health care service provided in person.

(7) This section does not require a health carrier to reimburse:

(a) An originating site for professional fees;

(b) A provider for a health care service that is not a covered benefit under the plan; or

(c) An originating site or health care provider when the site or provider is not a contracted provider under the plan.

(8) For purposes of this section:

(a) "Distant site" means the site at which a physician or other licensed provider, delivering a professional service, is physically located at the time the service is provided through telemedicine;

(b) "Health care service" has the same meaning as in RCW 48.43.005;

(c) "Hospital" means a facility licensed under chapter 70.41, 71.12, or 72.23 RCW;

(d) "Originating site" means the physical location of a patient receiving health care services through telemedicine;

(e) "Provider" has the same meaning as in RCW 48.43.005;

(f) "Store and forward technology" means use of an asynchronous transmission of a covered person's medical information from an originating site to the health care provider at a distant site which results in medical diagnosis and management of the covered person, and does not include the use of audio-only telephone, facsimile or e-mail; and

(g) "Telemedicine" means the delivery of health care services through the use of interactive audio and video technology, permitting real-time communication between the patient at the originating site and the provider, for the purpose of diagnosis, consultation or treatment. For purposes of this section only, "telemedicine" does not include the use of audio-only telephone, facsimile or e-mail.

WEST VIRGINIA
(NONE)

WISCONSIN
(NONE)

WYOMING
(NONE)

Chapter 4

Emerging Legal and Ethical Issues in Telehealth

4.1 Medical Staff Issues

4.1.1 Credentialing and Privileging of Telemedicine Providers

As telemedicine continues to evolve, novel services and approaches to technology are becoming more readily available, requiring hospitals and other facilities that use telemedicine to evaluate the organization's ability to safely provide services on an ongoing basis. Both the site where the patient is located at the time of service (originating site) and the site where the physician or other licensed practitioner is located while providing the telemedicine services (distant site) evaluate performance of those services as part of privileging and as part of the reappraisal conducted at the time of reappointment, renewal, or revision of clinical privileges. The Medicare Conditions of Participation, The Joint Commission guidelines, and state law should all be taken into consideration when credentialing and privileging telemedicine providers.

According to the Medicare Conditions of Participation (COPs), a hospital must have an organized medical staff that operates under bylaws approved by the governing body, and which is responsible for the quality of medical care provided to patients by the hospital.[1] The medical staff must examine the credentials of all eligible candidates for medical staff membership and make recommendations to the governing body on the appointment of these candidates in accordance with state law, including scope-of-practice laws, and the medical staff bylaws, rules and regulations.[2]

The Joint Commission lists three options for telemedicine credentialing:[3]

1. Originating site fully privileges and credentials the practitioner;
2. Originating site uses credentialing information from the distant site (if the distant site is Joint Commission accredited);
3. Originating site uses the credentialing and privileging decision from the distant site to make a final privileging decision pursuant to specific conditions being met (credentialing by proxy).

State laws and regulations should be carefully reviewed to determine what state specific options are allowed. For example, California law makes no reference to credentialing by proxy and only explicitly provides for two options: (1) full credentialing by the originating site hospital; or (2) credentialing that utilizes information from the distant site hospital but requires independent decision making.[4]

Additionally, the COPs permit the third option (credentialing by proxy) only if the hospital's governing body ensures, through its written agreement with the distant site hospital, all of the following conditions are met: (i) the distant site hospital providing the telemedicine services is a

---

[1] 42 C.F.R. § 482.22.

[2] 42 C.F.R. § 482.22(a)(2).

[3] MS.13.01.01.

[4] Cal. Bus. & Prof. Code § 2290.5.

Medicare-participating hospital; (ii) the individual distant site physician or practitioner is privileged at the distant site hospital which provides a current list of the distant site physician's or practitioner's privileges to the originating site hospital; (iii) the individual distant site physician or practitioner holds a license issued or recognized by the State in which the originating site is located; and (iv) the originating site has evidence of an internal review of the distant site physician's or practitioner's performance of these privileges and sends the distant site hospital such performance information for use in the periodic appraisal of the distant site physician or practitioner. At a minimum, this information must include all adverse events that result from the telemedicine services provided by the distant site physician or practitioner to the originating site hospital's patients and all complaints the originating site hospital has received about the distant site physician or practitioner.[5]

The main advantages of relying upon information from the distant site and credentialing by proxy are the efficiencies to be gained. However, long-standing case law holds that hospitals may be held accountable to patients for damages stemming from negligent credentialing.[6] Negligence *per se* also could apply where a hospital violates a statute intended to protect the interests of patients. To date, credentialing "information" from the distant site has not been explicitly defined, but would likely include key information that was verified by the distant site, including state licensure, board certification, current affiliations, practice history, and peer references.

4.1.2 Medical Staff Bylaws

Health care organizations that rely upon information provided from a distant site to credential and privilege telemedicine practitioners should ensure their medical staff bylaws and credentialing and privileging policies are updated to include criteria for granting privileges and a procedure to apply the criteria.[7] Some considerations include which category of the medical staff distant site practitioners will join, their level of involvement in medical staff committees, and what procedural rights they will be given.

4.1.3 Peer Review Information Sharing Protections

As telemedicine practice expands, health care organizations and telemedicine entities should be mindful of maintaining peer review information in a manner that preserves peer review privileges under state law. Policies and procedures should be developed to monitor telemedicine practitioners and the sharing of internal review information so that the privacy of peer review and patient information is protected while information necessary to accurately credential and privilege is obtained.

4.2 Ethics and Liability Issues

4.2.1 Ethical Practice of Telemedicine Guidelines

After several years of work, the American Medical Association's (AMA) Council on Ethics and Judicial Affairs developed new guidelines for the ethical practice of telemedicine that were adopted by a vote of physicians from around the country. These guidelines were formally adopted by AMA in 2016, with the organization's announcement that it hoped physicians and the telemedicine industry would use the guidelines to ensure safe and effective digital physician-patient interaction.[8]

The guidelines emphasize that physicians engaging in telemedicine should uphold the same guidelines as in any other model of care. They must continue to put patient welfare above their own

---

[5] 42 C.F.R. § 482.22(a)(3)(i)–(iv).

[6] *E.g.*, *Elam v. College Park Hospital* 132 Cal.App.3d 332 (1982).

[7] 42 C.F.R. § 482.12(a)(8), (a)(9).

[8] *See* AMA Announcement of New Guidelines, https://www.ama-assn.org/ama-adopts-new-guidance-ethical-practice-telemedicine.

interests, provide competent and sufficient care, respect patient privacy, and ensure continuity of care. Under AMA guidelines, physicians have the right to use their discretion in the application of telemedicine technology when conducting diagnostic evaluations and prescribing therapy. The guidelines recommend that physicians using telemedicine should:

- Inform patients regarding the limitations of the technology;
- Advise patients on how to arrange for follow-up care;
- Encourage patients to inform their primary physician when they've been treated via telehealth;
- Support policies and initiatives that promote access to telehealth or telemedicine services for all patients who could benefit from receiving care electronically; and
- Protect patient privacy and confidentiality.

The guidelines also recognize that a coordinated effort across the profession is necessary to avoid the pitfalls of telemedicine. Active engagement should support ongoing refinement of telemedicine technologies and relevant standards, while also promoting initiatives that will help make needed technology more readily available to all patients who want to use telemedicine services.

4.2.2 The Physician-Patient Relationship

As a general rule of medical malpractice, a physician does not owe a duty to a patient unless a physician-patient relationship has been established. Traditionally, the foundation of the physician-patient relationship was the in-person encounter.[9] An in-person encounter allows the physician to meet the patient, emphasize patient history and create the basis for mutual trust and empathy.

The existence of the relationship becomes more questionable in common telemedicine encounters in which the patient and physician never meet each other, never have a conversation, and the remote physician merely interprets an x-ray or other diagnostic tool that later impacts the patient's subsequent treatment by another physician. The physician-patient relationship does not necessarily have to be established through an in-person interaction, although concerns may arise about the nature of the physician-patient relationship and the impact that it may have on the quality of care.[10]

According to the AMA, a physician-patient relationship may be formed through:

- A face-to-face examination—an exam using two-way, real-time audio and visual capabilities, like a videoconference—if a face-to-face encounter would be required for the same service in person;
- A consultation with another physician who has an ongoing relationship with the patient. The physician who has established a valid physician-patient relationship must agree to supervise the patient's care; or
- Meeting evidence-based telemedicine practice guidelines developed by major medical specialty societies, such as those of radiology or pathology, for establishing a patient-physician relationship.[11]

---

[9] Goold SD, Lipkin M. *The Doctor-Patient Relationship.* J GEN INTERN MED. 1999;14 (Suppl 1):S26–33. doi: 10.1046/j.1525-1497.1999.00267.x.

[10] Weiner M, Biondich P. *The Influence of Information Technology on Patient-Physician Relationships.* J GEN INTERN MED 2006;21(Suppl 1):S35–9.

[11] American Medical Association, Telemedicine Physician-Patient Relationship Chart, https://www.ama-assn.org/sites/default/files/media-browser/specialty%20group/arc/ama-chart-telemedicine-patient-physician-relationship.pdf.

Some potential exceptions to establishing the physician-patient relationship before the telemedicine services are provided include on-call, cross coverage situations, emergency medical treatment, and other exceptions that become recognized as meeting or improving the standard of care.[12]

4.2.3 Standard of Care

Assuming a physician-patient relationship is established, the standard of care to which the physician's care is compared to determine negligence is not always clear, even in traditional medical encounters. Some courts prefer using a local or community standard of care, while others use a national standard of care.[13]

Some states have created telemedicine-specific informed consent standards, privacy standards, and general telemedicine standards of care. This creates an additional heightened standard of care to which the physician's actions might be compared in a telemedicine negligence or malpractice dispute.

In addition to statutory and regulatory standards of care for telemedicine, some private organizations have created guidelines for standards of care for various types of telemedicine encounters.[14]

When performing a telemedicine malpractice risk analysis, some of the questions to consider include the following:

- In what state is the patient located?
- In what state is the physician located?
- Is the physician properly trained to use the telemedicine equipment and did the physician use the equipment properly?
- Did the physician fail to utilize available telemedicine technology which could have prevented injury to the patient?
- What traditional medical encounters are most similar to the telemedicine encounter in question?
- What state specific laws apply (i.e., statute of limitations, medical malpractice damages caps, medical licensure laws, standards of care, burden of proof, informed consent, prescribing, etc.)?
- Does the physician's malpractice insurance cover the telemedicine service in question?

---

[12] *Id.*

[13] *See* Jay M. Zitter, *Annotation, Standard of Care Owed to Patient by Medical Specialist as Determined by Local "Like Community," State, National, or Other Standards*, 18 A.L.R. 4th 603, 608-19 (1982).

[14] *See, i.e.*, American Telemedicine Association http://hub.americantelemed.org/resources/telemedicine-practice-guidelines; ATA Clinical Guidelines for Telepathology, Pantanowitz Liron, Dickinson Kim, Evans Andrew J., Hassell Lewis A., Henricks Walter H., Lennerz Jochen K., Lowe Amanda, Parwani Anil V., Riben Michael, Smith COL Daniel, Tuthill J. Mark, Weinstein Ronald S., Wilbur David C., Krupinski Elizabeth A., and Bernard Jordana. Telemedicine and e-Health. November 2014, 20(11): 1049-1056. doi:10.1089/tmj.2014.9976; ACR White Paper on Teleradiology Practice: A Report from the Task Force on Teleradiology Practice, Ezequiel Silva III, MD, et. al., J AM COLL RADIOL 2013; 10:575-585; American Academy of Dermatology Association Position Statement on Teledermatology (Approved by Board of Directors 2/22/02; Amended by BOD 5/22/04; 11/9/13; 8/9/14; 5/16/15; 5/7/16) https://www.aad.org/Forms/Policies/Uploads/PS/PS-Teledermatology.pdf.

4.2.4 Internet Prescribing

Potential liability is prevalent in the context of internet prescribing. Online prescribing or internet prescribing refers to a provider prescribing a drug to a patient based upon an interaction that has taken place online.[15] Where interaction occurs online, questions are raised regarding whether the provider has enough information to make an informed decision regarding treatment. In some states, a patient-provider relationship based solely on internet interactions is prohibited.

As discussed further in Chapter 2, The Ryan Haight Online Pharmacy Consumer Protection Act of 2008 prohibits dispensing controlled substances via the Internet without a valid prescription.[16] For a prescription to be valid, it must be issued for a legitimate medical purpose in the usual course of professional practice by a practitioner who has conducted at least one in-person medical evaluation of the patient or a covering practitioner.[17]

Controlled substances prescribed via telemedicine are under Drug Enforcement Agency (DEA)[18] jurisdiction. The DEA is targeting rogue online pharmacies for prosecution and shutting down websites that allow patients to obtain prescriptions for controlled substances simply by filling out a questionnaire.[19] Due to the high risk of abuse and danger to public health, state medical boards also have been active in enforcing against this practice and many medical boards have issued position statements regarding the use of internet prescribing.[20] For example, some states have adopted policies to prevent physicians from prescribing drugs based solely on online questionnaires.[21] These policies are targeted at preventing abuses of controlled substances and are not meant to interfere with legitimate telemedicine practices and uses of telehealth technologies.

4.2.5 Multiple Treating Practitioners

Where multiple physicians or licensed professionals are involved in a telemedicine encounter, operation of the telemedicine equipment by one physician or licensed professional may affect the treatment or diagnosis provided by the other physician or licensed professional involved in the encounter. The question of who actually has control over the care of the patient, and liability for negligence with regard to such care, is not as clear as in traditional medical encounters in which one doctor diagnoses or treats the patient in a face-to-face encounter. Traditional rules on joint and several liability will apply to telemedicine encounters in which more than one physician is involved and is found to be responsible for an indivisible injury to a patient during a single encounter.

4.2.6 Patient Abandonment

Physicians can be held liable for patient abandonment if the physician unilaterally severs the relationship with the patient without reasonable notice or without providing adequate alternative medical care at a time when there is a necessity of continuing medical attention.[22] Telemedicine encounters are often one-time encounters for a specific purpose. Failed communication between the

---

[15] Center for Connected Health Policy, Online Prescribing, *available at* http://www.cchpca.org/online-prescribing-0.

[16] H.R. 6353, Public Law 110-425; 21 U.S.C. 829(e).

[17] *Id.*

[18] The DEA is the federal agency responsible for enforcement of the Controlled Substance Act (CSA).

[19] Drug Enforcement Administration, Report Suspected Unlawful Sales of Pharmaceutical Drugs on the Internet (Consumer Alert) *See* https://www.deadiversion.usdoj.gov/consumer_alert.htm.

[20] Federation of State Medical Boards, Internet Prescribing Enforcement Actions, *available at* https://www.fsmb.org/Media/Default/PDF/FSMB/Advocacy/Internet_Prescribing_Table.pdf.

[21] Federation of State Medical Boards, Internet Prescribing Law, *available at* https://www.fsmb.org/Media/Default/PDF/Advocacy/InternetPrescribinglaw.pdf.

[22] *King v. Fisher*, 918 S.W.2d 108, 112 (Tex. App.–Fort Worth 1996).

consulting or referring physician's roles in the ongoing care of the patient could result in an unintentional patient abandonment case in which both physicians assumed the other was responsible for the ongoing care of the patient.

Therefore, physicians involved in telemedicine encounters should establish policies and procedures to ensure proper communication to the patient and among the involved physicians regarding the ongoing care of the patient after the encounter.

4.2.7 Miscellaneous Negligence Issues

Another complicating malpractice issue for telemedicine is whether a physician will be held liable for not utilizing available telemedicine technologies. In certain circumstances, telemedicine use (e.g., remote patient monitoring during procedures) is becoming the standard of care. Further, physicians may be liable for improper use and lack of training to use telemedicine equipment properly.

4.2.8 Malpractice Insurance Coverage

Another issue to consider is whether the physician's malpractice insurance covers multi-state telemedicine encounters. Insurance risks vary from state to state. Further, some policies may only cover malpractice claims only in the state in which the physician is licensed to practice, or the state in which the policy was issued. Physicians should confirm coverage with their malpractice carriers prior to engaging in telemedicine practice.

4.3 Fraud and Abuse

As with any method for practicing medicine in the United States, a physician undertaking a telemedicine endeavor is subject to a multitude of complex federal and state health care fraud and abuse statutes, regulations, and case law. In general, the majority of fraud and abuse issues unique to telemedicine relate to the infrastructure, equipment, and support necessary to implement any effective telemedicine endeavor.

4.3.1 Federal Anti-Kickback Law

Under the anti-kickback statute, it is a criminal offense to knowingly and willfully offer, pay, solicit, or receive any remuneration to induce referrals of items or services reimbursable by any federal health care program.[23] If an arrangement that would otherwise implicate the anti-kickback statute meets all of the requirements of an applicable anti-kickback safe harbor, then the arrangement would not implicate the statute.[24] Two exceptions apply to situations relating to electronic prescribing items and services and electronic health records items and services, each subject to a list of conditions.[25]

The Office of Inspector General (OIG) is responsible for enforcing the anti-kickback statute and publishes various guidance documents to assist health care entities in determining whether a certain arrangement would implicate the anti-kickback statute. The OIG has published a number of advisory opinions and a special fraud alert addressing telemedicine-related fraud issues.[26]

---

[23] 42 U.S.C. § 120a-7b.

[24] 42 C.F.R. § 1001.952.

[25] 42 C.F.R. § 1001.952(x) and (y).

[26] Office of the Inspector General, Special Fraud Alert; Arrangements for the Provision of Clinical Lab Service, 59 Fed. Reg. 65,372, 65,377 (Dec. 19, 1994); 98 Op. Off. Inspector Gen. 18 (Nov. 25, 1998); 99 Op. Off. Inspector Gen. 14 (Dec. 28, 1999); 03 Op. Off. Inspector Gen. 04 (Feb. 12, 2003); 11 Op. Off. Inspector Gen. 12 (Sept. 6, 2011).

4.3.2 Federal Stark Law

The federal Stark self-referral law prohibits physicians from referring Medicare beneficiaries to an entity with which the physician has a financial relationship for designated health services reimbursable by Medicare, unless an exception applies.[27] The Stark self-referral prohibition is narrower in scope than the anti-kickback statute, but it is a strict liability offense that does not require intent. Compliance with a Stark exception protects a physician from violating the self-referral prohibition.[28]

A number of Stark law exceptions exist which could be relevant to telemedicine. For example, exceptions for electronic prescribing items and services and electronic health records items and services exist subject to certain specific conditions.[29] In addition, an exception for medical staffing incidental benefits also exists, providing that compensation in the form of low value items or services (e.g., pagers, internet access) offered to all medical staff and utilized while on hospital campus and reasonably related to the provision of medical services are not considered prohibited remuneration.[30] Many other self-referral exceptions would also work well with common telemedicine programs. Another exception is for community-wide health information systems, which permits physicians to refer Medicare patients to entities from which the physician has received information technology equipment or services that allow physician access to and sharing of electronic health records for patients served by community providers, if certain conditions are met.[31]

4.3.3 False Claims Act and Civil Monetary Penalties

Specific health care fraud and abuse violations, such as violations of the anti-kickback statute and Stark self-referral law, are often coupled with sanctions under the False Claims Act (FCA) and the Civil Monetary Penalties (CMP) authority of the OIG. The FCA prohibits knowingly submitting or causing to be submitted false or fraudulent claims for payment or false statements or certifications to the government.[32] CMPs are applicable if a person knowingly presents, or causes to be presented, to a state or federal government employee or agent, any false or improper claims.[33] The United States Supreme Court recently determined the implied certification theory can be a potential basis for liability under the FCA where certain conditions are satisfied.[34]

4.3.4 State Fraud and Abuse Laws

The federal fraud and abuse statutes and regulations are only the starting point for a telemedicine program fraud and abuse analysis. Any telemedicine program will also be subject to any state versions of fraud and abuse laws for the states into which the telemedicine program may reach.[35]

Some states have chosen to establish health care fraud and abuse laws that are much more expansive than the federal laws (e.g., applicable to all payors), while other states have chosen not to regulate the area at all. Certain states have chosen to integrate the federal fraud and abuse statutes

---

[27] 42 U.S.C. § 1395nn.

[28] *Id.*; 42 C.F.R. §§ 411.355-411.357.

[29] 42 C.F.R. § 411.357(v) and (w).

[30] 42 C.F.R. § 411.357(m).

[31] 42 C.F.R. § 411.357(u).

[32] 31 U.S.C. § 3729.

[33] 42 U.S.C. § 1320a-7a(a).

[34] *Universal Health Services, Inc. v. United States ex rel Escobar*, 136 S.Ct. 1989 (2016).

[35] *Summary of Fraud and Abuse Statutes and Regulations (50 State Survey)*, American Health Lawyers Association: Fraud and Abuse Practice Group, West Virginia Section Prepared by: Caleb P. Knight and Robert L. Coffield, Flaherty Sensabaugh Bonasso PLLC, March 8, 2013.

into their state Medicaid statutes even though the federal anti-kickback and self referral statutes already apply to all state Medicaid programs as the federally-subsidized health care programs. State fee-splitting laws and insurance laws should be considered for telehealth arrangements.

Some states have explicitly adopted certain aspects of the federal statutes but have failed to incorporate the related safe harbors and exceptions.[36] Therefore, an arrangement that complies with a federal exception may still be subject to state fraud and abuse sanctions. In addition, some states have telemedicine specific fraud and abuse laws, such as Kentucky[37] and Texas.[38]

4.4 Corporate Practice of Medicine

An often-overlooked barrier to the adoption of telehealth programs are state prohibitions on the corporate practice of medicine. The corporate practice of medicine doctrine generally prohibits unlicensed individuals and entities owned by laypersons from employing a licensed physician for the purpose of providing medical services or owning an interest in a medical practice.[39] The rationale for this prohibition is largely based on public policy considerations; namely, the concern that an unlicensed person or entity employing or controlling a physician's compensation could interfere with that physician's exercise of independent medical judgment, thereby undermining the physician-patient relationship.

State-specific rules relating to the corporate practice of medicine vary.[40] Some states, such as California, strictly prohibit physicians from engaging in the practice of medicine through a non-licensed corporate structure, whereas states such as Florida permit the practice of medicine by physicians as employees of a Florida corporation or partnership.[41] Other states, such as Hawaii and Ohio, have no prohibition whatsoever. In practice, many states permit professional service entities, such as professional corporations or professional limited liability companies, to practice medicine, but often require the entity be owned entirely by physicians licensed within the state.[42] For these reasons, telehealth providers need to be sure to also take the doctrine into consideration when developing business models within each state in which they plan to operate.

4.5 Privacy and Security Issues in Telehealth

Issues regarding privacy and security in the medical realm are not necessarily different in telehealth. However, because of the nature of the data—specifically, the novel formats not previously considered part of the patient's medical record, including audio/video recordings or remote monitoring data—and the ways in which it is used, privacy and security issues can pose challenges unique to the telehealth setting.

Whether delivering telemedicine services through telehealth technologies or in-person, providers are still required to comply with the federal and state privacy and security requirements. At the federal level, the Health Insurance Portability and Accountability Act of 1996 (HIPAA) requires the protection and secure handling of specific patient health information by covered entities, including

---

[36] Patric Hooper, *Practical Considerations for Defending Health Care Fraud and Abuse Cases*, in Health Care Fraud and Abuse: Practical Perspectives 214 (Linda A. Baumann, et al., eds. ABA Health Law Section, 2002), updated annually.

[37] Ky. Rev. Stat. § 311.5975.

[38] Tex. Occ. Code § 153.004.

[39] Depending on the state, authority for a prohibition of corporate practice of medicine may come from statute, regulations, case law, state Attorney General opinion, or state Medical Board opinions.

[40] *See AHLA Corporate Practice of Medicine: A Fifty State Survey*, Stuart Silverman (LexisNexis 2014).

[41] Cal. Bus. & Prof. Code §§ 2052, 2400; In re: Petition for Declaratory Statement of Conrad Goulet, M.D., Case No. 89-COM-01 (1989); Fla. Stat. § 458.

[42] *See, e.g.*, Cal. Corp. Code §§ 13400 *et seq.*; Ind. Code §§ 23-1.5 *et seq*; Kan. Stat. §§ 17-2706 *et seq.*

health care providers, clearinghouses, and health plans, including some employer-sponsored health plans.[43] Under HIPAA's Privacy Rule, providers and their associates who are covered by HIPAA must develop and stick to procedures that protect and secure protected health information (PHI) whenever it is received, handled, transferred, or shared—including electronically. Additionally, the Security Rule sets the standards for securing patient data that is stored or transferred by electronic methods.

Many states have also developed their own privacy and security laws, some of which are broader in scope than HIPAA.[44] For example, California's Confidentiality of Medical Information Act (CMIA) dictates rules for permissible uses and disclosures of medical information. In the past, the California law applied to the type of companies commonly subject to HIPAA—health care providers, health plans, and businesses that contract with these entities for work that involves access to medical information.[45] However, the law was recently amended to expand its scope to apply to mobile health application developers. Additionally, some states have enacted data security laws applicable specifically to telehealth providers.[46]

Providers utilizing telehealth should take steps to ensure that the environment where the telehealth interaction takes place, both at the originating and distant site, is secure and that no PHI is inadvertently exposed or vulnerable to third party interference, signal errors, or transmission outages. These types of incidents could result in data loss, miscommunications, or alteration of clinical information, all of which subject providers to liability risk as well as potential violations under HIPAA or state law.[47] As such, encryption and other security features are integral in complying with privacy and security laws.[48]

Ultimately, in order to ensure compliance at both the federal and state levels, telehealth providers will need to adapt their privacy and security practices in response to the specific privacy and security risks and challenges associated with the various forms of telehealth they utilize.

4.6 Mobile Health Technology

Mobile health is a fast growing space that is rapidly transforming the health care industry. Due to the increasing popularity of mobile devices and tablets, health care providers and patients alike have been turning to mobile technology to meet health care needs. Also known as "mHealth," mobile health is the use of portable devices, such as smart phones or tablets for health care purposes.[49] Users interface with the device by using an "app," which is an application that is downloaded to the device. Apps have been developed with a variety of features, including those that allow users to monitor health conditions; connect with providers; and even assist with medical diagnosis.

---

[43] 45 C.F.R. pt. 164. The Office of Civil Rights of the Department of Health and Human Services (OCR) is responsible for implementing and enforcing the privacy and security provisions of HIPAA.

[44] *See, e.g.*, Confidentiality of Medical Information Act, Cal. Civ. Code; §§ 56 *et seq.*; 210 Ill. Comp. Stat. 85/6.17; Wis. Stat. § 146.82.

[45] Cal. Civ. Code; § 56.06.

[46] Alabama, for example, requires telehealth providers to adopt protocols to authenticate and authorize users, authenticate the origin of information, and prevent unauthorized access. *See* Ala. Admin. Code r. 540-X-15-.06.

[47] *Case Examples Organized by Covered Entity*, U.S. DEP'T OF HEALTH & HUMAN SERVS., https://www.hhs.gov/hipaa/for-professionals/compliance-enforcement/examples/by-entity/index.html#2generalhospital.

[48] For guidance on facilitating the electronic exchange of health information in compliance with HIPAA's Privacy Rule, *see Health Information Technology*, U.S. DEP'T OF HEALTH & HUMAN SERVS., https://www.hhs.gov/hipaa/for-professionals/special-topics/health-information-technology/index.html.

[49] There are many agency definitions of "mHealth." For example, the World Health Organization defines mHealth as "an area of electronic health (eHealth) and it is the provision of health services and information via mobile technologies such as mobile phones and Personal Digital Assistants (PDAs)." *See* http://www.who.int/goe/publications/goe_mhealth_web.pdf.

4.6.1 FDA Regulation of Health Care Mobile Applications

The U.S. Food and Drug Administration (FDA) has been active in the regulation of mobile health and technology, and recognizes the extensive variety of actual and potential functions of mobile apps. However, not all health related apps are subject to FDA regulation. The FDA is primarily focused on apps that transform a user's mobile platform into a regulated medical device.

The guidance issued by the FDA in 2015 outlined when mobile medical apps would be subject to agency regulation:

- Products that will be regulated. These apps could harm a patient if they don't function correctly—for example, an app that calculates the radiation dosage for a cancer patient. These products require clinical validation prior to approval.
- Products for which the agency will exercise "enforcement discretion." FDA regulations still apply to these apps, but the FDA has chosen not to enforce them at this time because the products are lower-risk. An example is a simple diary app that allows patients to log and organize their health data.
- Products that will not be regulated. These apps might be used by patients or providers but aren't classified as medical devices—for example, an app that determines billing codes for reimbursement of health care visits.[50]

4.6.2 Other Federal Agency Regulation

Other federal agencies are also involved in the regulation of mobile technologies.

The Federal Communications Commission (FCC) establishes regulations regarding interstate and international communications.[51] With respect to mobile technology, the FCC authorizes a wide variety of radio frequency based medical devices, such as implanted devices and patient monitoring devices. The FCC also authorizes wireless carriers whose networks are used by a wide variety of mobile devices to access, store and transmit health information.

The Federal Trade Commission (FTC) establishes regulations regarding false, misleading and deceptive trade practices and provides a framework for mobile privacy. It is responsible for enforcing numerous statutes, including the Federal Trade Commission Act.[52]

The Office of Civil Rights of the Department of Health & Human Services (OCR) is responsible for implementing and enforcing the privacy and security provisions of the Health Insurance Portability and Accountability Act of 1996 (HIPAA).[53] HIPAA protects individuals' personal health information, which may be transmitted when using health based mobile apps.

The Office of the National Coordinator for Health Information Technology (ONC) is responsible coordination of nationwide efforts to implement and use the most advanced health information technology and the electronic exchange of health information.[54]

Several of these agencies have worked together to provide further guidance for mobile app developers. On April 5, 2016, the FTC, in conjunction with HHS, the FDA, OCR, and ONC, released a new web-based interactive tool to assist mobile health app developers in navigating

---

[50] FDA, "Mobile Medical Applications—Guidance for Industry and Food and Drug Administration Staff" (February 9, 2015) *available at* https://www.fda.gov/downloads/MedicalDevices/.../UCM263366.pdf.

[51] See https://www.fcc.gov/about-fcc/what-we-do.

[52] *See* https://www.ftc.gov/enforcement/statutes.

[53] *See* https://www.hhs.gov/hipaa/for-professionals/compliance-enforcement/.

[54] *See* https:/www.healthit.gov/newsroom/about-onc.

applicable federal laws and regulations in the areas of advertising and marketing, medical devices, and data security and privacy.[55] The tool guides developers through a series of questions about who they are, what kind of app they are developing and how much data their app will collect. The tool then analyzes these answers to provide information about various relevant laws, including the FTC Act, the FTC's Health Breach Notification Rule, HIPAA, and the FD&C Act. However, the FTC's website includes a disclaimer that the web-based tool is "not meant to be legal advice about all of your compliance obligations, but it will provide a snapshot of a few important laws and regulations from three federal agencies."[56] Mobile app developers are thus cautioned to consult with counsel to determine the laws and rules applicable to the specific technology at issue.

---

[55] Mobile Health Apps Interactive Tool, *available at* https://www.ftc.gov/tips-advice/business-center/guidance/mobile-health-apps-interactive-tool.

[56] *Id.*

INDEX

INDEX

[References are to sections.]

[References are to sections.]